Grow your own
Bushfoods

Keith and Irene Smith

NEW
HOLLAND

Published in Australia by
New Holland Publishers (Australia) Pty Ltd
Sydney • Auckland

National Library of Australia Cataloguing-in-Publication Data:
Smith, Keith, 1939–.
Grow your own bushfoods.
Bibliography.
Includes index.

ISBN 9781864364590.
1. Cookery (Wild foods). 2. Wild foods - Australia.
2. Wild plants, Edible - Australia. I. Smith, Irene, 1942–.
II. Norling, Beth. III. Title.
581.6320994

Commissioning Editor: Derelie Evely
Project co-ordinator: Julie Nekich
Editor: Brenda Little
Designer: Jo Waite
Front cover design: Lorena Susak
Illustrator: Beth Norling
Production Director: Olga Dementiev

Cover photograph: Top: Pincushion Hakea (shutterstock); Bottom; Lilly pilly (Elizabeth
Richardson)

Keep up with New Holland Publishers on Facebook
www.facebook.com/NewHollandPublishers

Contents

Preface

Austral doubah, bush tomatoes, Davidson plum, geebungs, lemon myrtle, lilly pilly, midyimberry, riberry, quandong, warrigal greens and wattleseed are all indigenous food-bearing plants which grow in the bush or the outback, but imagine going into your own garden and picking them to eat! In this book we tell you how to grow and harvest 150 kinds of Aussie bushfoods right in your own backyard.

We've always been organic gardeners, conscious of the fragility of our environment. Growing bushfoods is a logical step in thinking globally and acting locally. Over the last couple of years we've researched intensively and familiarised ourselves with Aussie bushfoods, seeking the best ones for home gardeners, both from the point of view of growing and eating. Our trip to Central Australia in 1998, when Aborigines took us through their communities and shared fruits with us straight from the trees, helped us tie our ideas together.

Nothing could be more environmentally friendly than a bushfood garden. The plants belong here — they have already adapted to our harsh climate and poor soils. Once established in the garden, bushfood plants need little care; a bushfood garden is a low-maintenance garden.

Bushfoods are natural and organic. They don't need artificial fertilisers or pesticides; in fact many can be damaged or killed by them. Bushfood gardeners help to preserve endangered plant species.

A vast and rich array of indigenous plants have never been thought of as food plants and no one has tried to grow them. Seeds and seedlings of these plants have only recently become available from nurseries.

We found that most species have varieties to suit each climatic region, so it doesn't matter where you live, you have a range of plants from which to choose. We think most people will be delighted and amazed by the subtle flavours of lemon myrtle, pepperberry, wattleseed and many plants which can be used in the way we now use herbs and spices.

Bushfoods, especially bushfruits, are concentrated balls of energy and taste. They are only small, but contain plenty of goodness and flavour because, unlike introduced fruits and vegetables, there's very little water in them. They grow in places where there is very little or infrequent rain.

Think Italy—think pasta! Think India—think curry! Think Australia —now think bushfoods!

Food is an important part of a country's culture and we believe we're on the verge of creating a unique Australian cuisine. Bushfoods are already on the menu of many gourmet restaurants and some products are starting to appear in specialty shops and supermarkets.

Bushfoods have a bright future. In this new and rapidly growing primary industry there are opportunities for more growers to become involved. There are already plantations of quandong, pepperberry, muntries, cider gums and wattle trees. Small businesses are marketing jams, chutneys and dried herbs, spices and teas. Universities and research centres such as the CSIRO are trying to find the best bushfood varieties and ways to improve their size, taste and reliability.

Bushfoods are new to us, but not to Australian Aborigines. Their knowledge was acquired over 60 000 years in a process one botanist has described as 'eat, die and learn'. As much as 80 per cent of their food was gathered from plants. They had a name for each one and recognised at least five seasons in the year. The Eora (Sydney Aborigines) knew that the mullet were running when the golden wattle was in blossom. Aborigines used plants as food, medicine, tools, shelter and calendars.

Growing bushfoods is a wonderful way of learning about their culture and the environment. We dedicate this book to the Aborigines of Australia.

Keith and Irene Smith
Birchgrove, NSW

How to use this book

Most people have heard of Australian bush tucker and know it is collected from trees and plants in the wild. But the idea of growing your own bushfoods, just like ordinary fruits and vegetables, is new and fairly radical. *Grow Your Own Bushfoods* has been created to change all that.

The five major kinds of bushfoods—leaf flavours, fruits, vegetables and tubers, seeds and nuts, and nectar—are dealt with separately in the first five chapters. Some 70 bushfoods are introduced with plant profile panels, rather like an identikit which tells you what each plant looks like. Each lists the plant's common, botanical, Aboriginal and other names. Then come the vital statistics: the best climate in which the plant will grow successfully, where it is found in the wild, its form and height, foliage, flowers, colour, scent, fruit, fruit, pods, tubers or seeds, times of flowering and when it is rady to eat. About 40 plants have been illustrated by our artist Beth Norling.

A further 70 related species or varieties of these main plants are described more briefly. Some have different kinds of leaves, flowers or fruit, while others might be taller or shorter or suit distinct climatic niches.

Every plant profile is followed by growing directions and suggestions for the best ways to prepare and eat your bushfoods, for example, as a flavouring or in jam, muffins or sauces and how to make bush teas and sweet drinks. Boxes, with specific recipes, tips and hints and some of the ways in which Aboriginal people treated and used these foods are scattered throughout the book.

In Chapter 6, *Growing Bushfoods*, you will find a practical and detailed guide on growing bushfood plants, with emphasis on natural organic methods, free from chemical fertilisers or pesticides.

CHAPTER 1

Bushleaf Flavours

Fragrance and flavour ... Bushleaf flavours are best used like spices or herbs to give a subtle new taste to your dishes. They adapt easily to any style of cooking.

These plants have colourful blossoms and sweet-scented leaves and look wonderful in the garden. They can also be used to make aromatic hot or cold teas.

LEMON MYRTLE

Backhousia citriodora (syn. *B. citrodorus)*
Aboriginal names: Wom-bai (Qld)
Other names: Grey myrtle, lemon ironwood, lemon-scented myrtle,
neverbreak, Queensland myrtle, sweet verbena tree.

FAMILY	MYRTACEAE
CLIMATE	Temperate to subtropical
HABITAT	Coastal rainforests, from southern NSW to Fraser Island (Qld)
FORM	Dense shrub or compact evergreen tree, 3–8 m high and 3 m wide
FOLIAGE	Dark green elliptical leaves to 10 cm long, giving off strong lemon scent when crushed
FLOWERS	Profuse clusters of small, creamy white flowers, through summer

Lemon myrtle is a pleasant, versatile flavouring used with soups, main courses (especially fish) and desserts. It can be used fresh or dried, whole, shredded, or crushed into powder. You can now obtain it in supermarkets.

The dense, dull green foliage has a strong, long-lasting, pleasant perfume, like lemon or lemon verbena. The leaves contain *citral*, an essential oil which is used in perfumed soaps.

You can add lemon myrtle seeds and flowers to bush teas made from the leaves and in scented sachets.

In South Gippsland, Victoria and at Bangalow, New South Wales, some fifteen thousand trees have been planted to supply the strong commercial demand for lemon myrtle.

Growing

Lemon myrtles tolerate cool conditions, but are frost-tender. They should be grown in a warm, sheltered spot in low-frost areas, in fertile, well-drained soil.

The young trees prefer some shade, as in the wild they grow in sheltered spots along creek banks.

Cuttings and root suckers strike easily and flower sooner than seedlings. Seed is ripe in autumn and germinates well, but is very fine.

When sowing cover them lightly with sand. Young plants need to be watered regularly, mulched well and given the odd side-dressing of compost.

Lemon myrtle is ideal for a tall, scented hedge or privacy screen and does well as a backyard tree in the Sydney area. The scaly bark is a host for bush orchids.

Flavouring
Lemon myrtle leaves, flowers and seeds can be dried simply by hanging them in an airy, sheltered, shady place. Store in an airtight container.

The lemon flavour is good in sorbets and custards, and superb with fish. Sprinkle over fish before grilling or stir powdered lemon myrtle into mayonnaise to make a tangy bushfood *sauce tartare* to serve with fried fish. Use whole lemon myrtle leaves, fresh or dried, in sauces or vinegar and to flavour jellies made from riberries and other bushfruits. When Asian recipes call for lemon grass use fresh or powdered lemon myrtle leaves. Sprinkle ground lemon myrtle on freshly baked bread, pumpkin or other vegetable soups and seafood chowder.

Tea time
Make lemon myrtle tea by infusing half a dozen whole fresh leaves in a small teapot. Add a few flower buds if you have them. This refreshing brew is pale green, like lemon or lime, and has the same aroma. You can also make tea from lemon myrtle powder. Leave to cool and serve iced. Try a few lemon myrtle leaves in homemade lemonade.

RELATED PLANTS
Aniseed myrtle (*Backhousia anisata*)
Aniseed myrtle is native to southern Queensland and northern New South Wales and will grow as far south as Melbourne, Victoria. These large, bushy trees may reach 10 to 25 m in height. They have shiny green leaves with wavy margins and in spring clusters of glossy, fluffy white flowers with a strong aniseed scent.

Propagate by sowing whole seed-bearing fruits while they are fresh and green. Plants prefer fertile, well-composted soil.

Crushed leaves have a strong aniseed flavour and smell like liquorice. They are used in the same way as lemon myrtle, but in smaller amounts as their taste is pungent and stimulating.

MOUNTAIN PEPPER

Tasmannia lanceolata
(syn. *Drimys lanceolata*)
Dioecious
Aboriginal name: Mourao (NSW)
Other names: Native pepper,
pepperberries, pepper bush,
pepper shrub, pepper tree,
Tasmanian mountain pepper

FAMILY	WINTERACEAE
CLIMATE	Cool temperate
HABITAT	Cool, moist gullies in mountain forests (800–1200 m) of south-east Australia from Tas to the Blue Mountains (NSW)
FORM	Small shrub, 2–3 m high, spreading 2 m, with dark red stems
FOLIAGE	Dark green, shiny, narrow, spear-shaped, aromatic leaves, 4–8 cm long. Can be picked all year
FLOWERS	Creamy white male and female flowers, 1–2 cm across, in bunches on separate trees, spring and summer
FRUITS	Rounded, pea-sized, purple-black berries ripen on female plants in autumn

Most of us use pepper every day, so why not use native pepperberries?

When dried and ground and sprinkled over food, these small, pea-sized berries have a sharp, hot, spicy flavour, stronger and more aromatic than true pepper (*Piper nigrum*). Packets of ground native pepper are now widely available.

Leaf Vinegars

Use 5 to 10 g of leaves of lemon myrtle or mountain pepper to each 1 litre of good quality white vinegar.

Bring to the boil and simmer for about 20 minutes.

Strain into sterile jars or bottles, put in a sprig of the plant for decoration, seal and store.

Use these vinegars in salad dressings or for pickling.

Growing

Native pepper plants are either male or female, but only the female plant yields pepperberries, so you must plant at least one of each sex. Pepperberries will not grow in dry or windy conditions, or in hot summer weather. Plants are frost-hardy.

Fresh seed may take two months or more to germinate. Cuttings taken in autumn strike readily. Plants grow slowly, but are adaptable. They need well-composted, well-drained soil and ample water and cannot tolerate very hot summers or dry periods until they are growing strongly.

Peppers are easy to harvest once they are well established. Leaves can be picked all year.

Flavouring

Pepperberries have become a prized ingredient in Australian bushfood cooking. They have a stronger, 'hot' taste than black peppers, so use them more sparingly.

When harvested, the berries are left to dry until wrinkled and hard. They are larger than the usual peppercorns, but can be ground in some pepper grinders, or you may need the special ones made for larger berries now on the market. Store in an airtight container. The berries can also be pickled in brine.

Try pepperberries in Asian curry and chilli dishes, salad dressings, marinades and pickles, or grind over chicken or steak. They go particularly well with cheese, bread and pate.

Pepperberry leaves are aromatic when crushed and can be used fresh or dried. Add whole leaves to stews and casseroles, but only in the last half hour of cooking because of their strong flavour, and remove them before serving. Store leaves in airtight containers to retain their aroma. Crumble up dried leaves by hand, or mill them into a fine powder. The flower buds are edible and can be added to salads or pickled.

RELATED PLANTS

Dorrigo pepper (*Tasmannia stipitata;* syn. *Drimys stipitata*)
Also called northern pepperbush. A subtropical relative of mountain pepper, native to rainforests of the north coast of New South Wales and southern Queensland. Leaves (to 13 cm) are used in the same way as those of mountain pepper. Dark berries which ripen in autumn are dried, ground and used as pepper. Propagate from cuttings.

Alpine or snow pepper (*Tasmannia xerophila;* syn. *Drimys xerophila*)
A rounded, small berried shrub, 1 to 1.5 m high, with short, 2 to 7 cm long blunt, spicy, aromatic leaves that turn a reddish colour when dried. The plant is cold-tolerant and grows at high altitudes in alpine areas of southern Australia.

BUSH TEA LEAF
Ocimum tenuiflorum (syn. *Ocimum sanctum*)
Aboriginal names: Bulla bulla (Mitchell River, Qld), mooda (Cloncurry River, Qld), jali (Gurinji, NT)
Other names: Native basil or native thyme

FAMILY	LAMIACEAE
CLIMATE	Arid to tropical
HABITAT	Widespread, especially in northern Qld and NT
FORM	Perennial herb to 30 cm in height, with woody, branching stems
FOLIAGE	Greyish, broad, spear-shaped hairy leaves, with a pungent mint scent, to 5 cm long
FLOWERS	Tiny purple or white mint flowers in late winter and spring

Native thyme is related to the Indian sacred basil (*Ocimum sanctum*). The German explorer Ludwig Leichhardt called the plant 'wild marjoram', and used the leaves to make tea and added them to soup.

Strangely, plants growing in northern Australia are said to have an odour similar to anise, while those in eastern Australia smell like cloves.

Growing
This basil is easily raised from seed (plant in late spring) or cuttings and grows in the same way as any kind of mint or basil. Once established, bushes need little watering and will last up to 10 years. Leaves can be cut several times a week, ideally in the early morning. Like basil, bush tea leaf is a beneficial 'companion plant' for tomatoes.

The volatile oils and fragrance of bush tea leaves, fresh or dried, will discourage flies, fleas, beetles and moths.

Flavouring
Use fresh leaves sparingly in salads, pasta sauces and salsas and for making fresh mint tea. Add fresh or dried leaves or powder to pep up

omlettes, fish, potato salad, sauce and soups. Dried leaves can also be used. Bush tea leaf, sold as 'Native thyme', is now available commercially dried and ground, and can be used in the same way as lemon myrtle.

Tea time
For a refreshing, clove-tasting bush tea, add a few dried leaves and stems to hot water and allow to steep. Aborigines crush the leaves in a container of water to make a medicinal 'cold tea' to prevent illness.

RELATED PLANTS
Hairy basil (*Ocimum americanum*)
Hairy basil is a form of bush basil which grows wild in Qld and northern Australia, but might be an introduced weed. The aromatic leaves are used to flavour curries and fish dishes. Seeds are soaked in water to make a drink and an essential oil is extracted from the plant.

RIVER MINT
Mentha australis (syn. *Mentha satureioides*)
Perennial
Aboriginal name: Panaryle (Coranderrk Station, Vic). Probably derived from the English pennyroyal (*Mentha pulegium*).
Other names: Native peppermint

FAMILY	LABIATAE
CLIMATE	Temperate
HABITAT	Widespread in swamps and on river banks except in arid areas
FORM	Slender, spreading herb with four-angled stems
FOLIAGE	Aromatic leaves, narrow, broad, or spear-shaped, 2–5 cm long
FLOWERS	Small white or mauve flowers in clusters in leaf axils

Growing
River mint is a pretty, upright herb which likes moist soil and weather. It will grow in damp places and in semi-shade under trees, as long as the soil is fertile. Plants are easily increased by cuttings or root division. Plant 60 cm apart. Transfer plants to fresh ground after four years.

Flavouring

Add river mint leaves to boiled peas, salads, jellies, desserts and sweet sauces, especially those based on chocolate. Sprinkle ground dried leaves over boiled peas or pea soup. River mint has a strong peppermint aroma and flavour and yields an oil similar to oil of peppermint (menthol), which is extracted from *Mentha piperita*.

Tea time

You can make a stimulating peppermint tea by pouring boiling water over a few sprigs of fresh river mint leaves to each cup. Leave to brew for 5 to 10 minutes. Add sugar and a squeeze of lemon juice to flavour.

Minty mouthwash

River mint tea is good for indigestion; cooled, it makes a fresh, antiseptic mouthwash.

CAPE BARREN TEA

Correa alba
Other names: Native fuchsia, white correa

FAMILY	RUTACEAE
CLIMATE	Temperate to cool temperate
HABITAT	Sand dunes and cliffs of the SE coast, from NSW to Tas and SA
FORM	Compact shrub, 1–2 m high, spreading 1.5–2 m
FOLIAGE	Grey-green, furry, rounded leaves, 2–4 cm long, hairy on the underside, with tiny oil dots; aromatic when crushed
FLOWERS	Small, waxy white (sometimes pink) star-shaped flowers, each with four curly petals, bloom all year, mainly in winter

Quaker missionary James Backhouse recognised large bushes of *Correa alba* covering the sandhills of the western head of the Tamar River when he was visiting George Town, Tas (then Van Diemens Land), in December 1833. Sealers living on the islands in Bass Strait, and Cape Barren Island in the Furneaux group, made a tea substitute from its leaves.

Growing

Cape Barren tea is a hardy coastal scented shrub which resists wind and salt spray and needs little watering once established.

It makes a very attractive ground cover for seaside gardens, and adapts to mountain areas, where it can tolerate shade and frost. Plants flower best in full sun.

Plants grow easily from seed, or from cuttings taken in early summer. The seeds shed from the green seed cases are difficult to collect. Plant in sandy or well-drained, light to medium soil.

Tea time

Tea made from the leaves of *Correa alba* tastes like jasmine tea and should be taken without milk.

RELATED PLANTS

Correa alba var. *rotundifolia*, a smaller, dense hairy bush, with starry flowers in winter, is found in south-west Victoria and south-east South Australia.

C. alba, 'Western Pink Star', is a prostrate, mounding shrub only 18 cm high with long-lasting bright pink flowers. It is thought to be extinct in the wild.

RUNNING POSTMAN

Kennedia prostrata
Aboriginal name: Kabin
(Coranderrk, Vic)
Other names: Red runner, creeping or scarlet coral pea, scarlet pea

FAMILY	PAPILIONACEAE
CLIMATE	Temperate
HABITAT	Open forests and sandy plains of SE and SW Australia
FORM	A sprawling, prostrate perennial creeper, forming a mat which can cover 1–3 m

FOLIAGE	Round, heart-shaped, broad, light green leaflets growing in threes on thin stems
FLOWERS	Scarlet, pea-like flowers, 2–2.5 cm long in spring and summer

The beautiful flowers of running postman have been described as 'butterflies on stems'. The name is said to come from the bright 'post-box' red pea-like flowers, marked with yellow, but we wonder if postmen delivering mail might have worn red caps in colonial times?

The genus is named after eighteenth century English nurseryman Lewis Kennedy.

Growing

Running postman is an attractive, quick-growing ground cover, whose stems form a tangled mat which can cover an area of several square metres in one season. This 'living mulch' will hold the soil together on steep banks. The flowering creepers will wind through long grass.

The plants resist light frost and dry spells and will grow in most soils, even in clay, though well-drained fertile soil is best. Choose a spot that is shaded for part of the day. Sow scarified seed in pots in spring, summer or autumn and transplant to permanent positions 1.5 m apart.

Prune back runners to prevent nearby shrubs becoming entangled. Mulch around the base of the plants in spring.

Tea time

Aborigines sucked nectar from the pea-like flowers and used the vines to make twine to lash together the ends of their bark canoes. Settlers soon found that they could brew up a substitute for tea from the sweet-tasting, shamrock-like leaves.

> We also found a plant which grew about the rocks & amongst the underwood entwined, the leaves of which boiled made a pleasant drink and was used as Tea by our Ships Company: It has much the taste of Liquorish [liquorice] & serves both for Tea & Sugar & is recommended as a very wholesome drink & a good thing to take to sea.
>
> William Bradley, *Journal*, Sydney, October 1788

SWEET TEA

Smilax glyciphylla

Aboriginal name: Bor'abor'adin (Kabi Kabi, Qld), warraburra (Eora, Sydney)

Other names: Botany Bay tea, native sarsaparilla, thornless smilax

FAMILY	SMILACACEAE
CLIMATE	Temperate
HABITAT	Moist eucalyptus forests from Ulladulla (NSW) to Qld
FORM	A vigorous shrubby creeper with wiry tendrils and prickly stems
FLOWERS	Tiny, white, pale green or purple in summer
FOLIAGE	Rounded, tapering, net-veined leaves, pale on the underside, 4–10 cm long
FRUITS	Clusters of small black berries, each with three hard, shiny seeds

Sweet tea or 'native sarsaparilla' grew around Botany Bay and Port Jackson and was used by Australia's first colonists to make a tea substitute. Its acrid taste contributed to its curative reputation. Convicts who went into the bush to collect sweet tea often became lost or were attacked by Aborigines.

In a letter to England, dated 'Sidney Town, 10 July 1788', Marine Private John Russell and his wife Elizabeth wrote: 'Since our arrival we have found several shrubs that serve as tea, greens &c. One sort of the teas sweetening the rest which I have heare sent some leaves as a sample.'

After his death a packet of 'Leaves from Botany Bay used as tea' was found among the papers of Dr Johnston's biographer, James Boswell. These *Smilax glyciphylla* leaves were a gift from Mary Bryant, who escaped from Sydney in 1792 with her husband, children and other convicts, and sailed to Timor in an open boat. Boswell helped Mary Bryant to obtain a free pardon in London.

In the late nineteenth century, sweet tea was sold by Sydney herbalists.

Keith's mother remembers that her grandfather, John Bede Bugden, a jobbing gardener who had been a farmer at Camden in NSW, often went into the bush on Sundays to collect 'sarsaparilla' vines. He brought the leaves back to his home at North Strathfield in Sydney and boiled them into syrup for a tonic tea.

The true or 'Jamaican' sarsaparilla (*Smilax officinalis*) is native to tropical Central America. A tonic tea or soft drink made from its root was popular in the United States.

Growing

Unlike its close relative, the lawyer vine (*Smilax australis*), stems of the sweet tea vine do not have prickles.

Plants will grow in most kinds of soil and are propagated from cuttings. Train vines to climb a trellis or low fence in semi or full shade. Southern types are frost-hardy.

Flavouring

Sweet tea leaves are sweet and astringent, taste like liquorice root and are refreshing to chew. Aborigines chewed the leaves and ate the ripe berries raw. On analysis, the berries show traces of a mild narcotic and a high vitamin C content.

Tea time

The first settlers used sweet tea as a tonic and an antiscorbutic. It became a famous bush medicine which was supposed to cure pains in the stomach and to prevent scurvy, coughs and chest troubles.

To make a tea, use a handful of leaves to each 1 litre of boiling water. Steep the leaves in the same way as ordinary tea. Drink sweet tea hot or iced, or let it cool and store in bottles. It has a strong, bitter-sweet taste, so there is no need to add sugar. A few leaves can be added to marinades for meat.

Teas from trees

Trees and shrubs of both *Leptospermum* and *Melaleuca* species have been known since 1773, when their leaves were used by Captain James Cook's sailors as a substitute for tea. Melaleucas today are more often called paperbarks and honey myrtles.

LEPTOSPERMUM
FAMILY MYRTACEAE

In August and September 1788 at Adventure Bay (Tas), during William Bligh's voyage on the HMS *Bounty*, botanist David Nelson and gardener William Brown gathered leaves from tea-trees to make a tea substitute. The sailors used old dry branches as brooms for sweeping the ship's decks. Early settlers in Australia found the aromatic leaves of leptospermums the best substitute for tea.

There are about 80 species of leptospermum. They grow from New Zealand to Malaysia. The shrubs and small trees, typically multi-stemmed, grow 3–8 m in height, in swampy places, mainly in the southern states of the Australian continent.

The dried brush is now used to make tea-tree fences.

Growing

Leptospermums grow well on poorly-drained heavy coastal soils or on better soils inland and in the mountains if there is little frost. Plants are more sensitive to frost when young. Unlike most Australian plants, they thrive in swampy, acidic conditions. Light, moist soils are ideal.

Set out plants in a sunny or partly-shaded spot. They are likely to grow into more compact trees if planted in full sun.

The seed is very fine and should be sown sparsely in spring (cover with sand). Transplant the seedlings when large enough to handle. Tip cuttings strike well.

The trees are hardy, adaptable and fast-growing, happy on the coast, and in swamps, or mountains and in milder, moister inland areas. They are short-lived and reach their maximum height in three or four years. Tea-trees make a thick hedge or screen when trimmed and can be coppiced or used as street trees if the lower branches are cut.

LEMON SCENTED TEA-TREE
Leptospermum petersonii (syn. *Leptospermum citratum*)

CLIMATE	Temperate to subtropical
HABITAT	Wet forests and rainforests of NSW and Qld.
FORM	Large, rounded evergreen shrub or tree, about 2–5 m high and wide

| FOLIAGE | Small, narrow, flat, pale green leaves, 2.5–3.5 cm long, containing an aromatic oil |
| FLOWERS | Masses of single, small white flowers in spring and early summer |

A strong lemon fragrance is given off by the crushed leaves, which contain *citral* and *citronellal*. Botanist W. J. Peterson collected the type specimen in 1905.

Tea time

Lemon-scented tea-tree leaves can be used alone or mixed with other leaf teas. The tasty tea gives off a beautiful aroma. Add a few leaves to the pot when making ordinary tea.

'With a little persistence, one could probably become fond of tea-tree tea', wrote A.B. and J.W. Cribb in *Wild Food in Australia* (1974).

The Aussie mozzie blocker

Dusk … and pesky mosquitoes buzz into your backyard looking for victims, just as you light up the barbecue! Don't worry, an Australian shrub will protect you!

The fine, narrow, lemon-scented leaves of the olive tea-tree (*Leptospermum liversidgei*) are a living, natural mosquito repellent. They continually release *citronella*, which blocks the carbon dioxide signals released by humans and warm-blooded animals, and which attract mosquitoes.

This ability was discovered by Melbourne author and horticulturalist Bill Molyneux of Austraflora, who coined the name 'Mozzie blocker'. Bill wholesales plants to nurseries around Australia.

Olive tea trees have small white or pink flowers, often produced on old wood.

Growing

The plant grows in temperate to subtropical climates and is native to coastal swamps of northern NSW and Qld. It is an upright shrub, 1–2 m high and 1 m wide. Propagate by seed or cuttings.

Plants grow well in light soil in coastal areas, but adapt to any climate if kept well-watered. Space plants 2 m apart.

MANUKA

Leptospermum scoparium
Other names: Broom tea-tree

CLIMATE   Temperate to tropical
HABITAT   Coastal SE Australia, from Tas to Qld; also New Zealand
FORM   Erect, broom-like shrub, reaching 3–6 m in height
FOLIAGE   Shiny, dark green, small, narrow, pointed leaves, about 1 cm long
FLOWERS   White, sometimes tinged pink, about 1 cm in diameter, massed along stems, in spring and summer

Leptospermums were first called tea-trees when Captain James Cook's crew aboard HMS *Resolution* at Dusky Sound, New Zealand, in 1773 drank tea made from the leaves of manuka as a remedy against scurvy. Anders Sparrman, a Swedish naturalist on board the ship, liked to mix up a brew of manuka with rum and brown sugar.

Australian botanist Joseph Maiden (1889) said 'the taste of the infusion made from them is too aromatic for the European palate'. Mixed with spruce leaves, Manuka takes away the astringent taste in home brewed beer.

RELATED PLANTS

Leptospermum scoparium var. *rotundifolium*
An erect shrub, 1 to 3 m high, native to the Australian and New Zealand coast and the Blue Mountains of NSW, with rounded leaves, 6 to 8 cm across and pink flowers with a green centre. Plants thrive in well-drained acid to neutral soil and can be lightly pruned to shape after flowering.

About thirty-five varieties of manuka have been developed in New Zealand; most are hybrids with pink to red flowers.

TANTOON

Leptospermum flavescens
Aboriginal name: Tantoon (Bundaberg, Qld)
Other names: Swamp tea-tree

CLIMATE   Temperate to subtropical
HABITAT   Coastal heaths and woodlands from Tas to Qld
FORM   Erect shrub, with drooping branches, 1–3 m tall and 3 m wide

FOLIAGE   Light green, narrow, flat, stiff, blunt, aromatic leaves, 1–2 cm long

FLOWERS   Single, cream or yellow-green, sweet-scented flowers, often with wavy petals.

The paperbark poet

In 1988, during Australia's Bicentenary, poet Kath Walker changed her name to Oodgeroo Noonucal to identify more closely with her Aboriginal heritage. Oodgeroo is the name given to the white paperbark or weeping tea-tree (*Melaleuca leucadendron*) by her people, the Noonual, of Stradbroke Island, Qld. It grows in salty swamps, gullies, along streams and has 'waterproof' bark.

We gathered some blossoms of the drooping tea-tree, which were full of honey, and, when soaked, imparted a very agreeable sweetness to the water. We frequently observed great quantities of washed blossoms of this tree in the deserted camps of the natives; showing that they were as fond of the honey in the blossoms of the tea-tree, as the natives of the east coast are of that of the several species of Banksia.

Ludwig Leichhhardt, *Journal of an Overland Expedition in Australia*, London, 1847

MELALEUCA
FAMILY MYRTACEAE

Melaleucas, once called tea-trees, are now called paperbark trees. They are valued for their soft, white, paper-like bark, which peels off easily. Some species, which emit a strong perfume, are called honey myrtles. There are about 200 species of melaleuca, most are native to Australia, and there are a few in New Zealand. They bear showy, spiky flowers like banksias or bottlebrushes.

Aborigines stripped off sheets of the soft, spongy bark to wrap up food to cook or to make containers for food and water. They also used it to make roof shelters, or to light fires and mend holes in their canoes.

The plants were collected near Sydney in 1793 by Spanish botanist Antonio Cavanilles. In the Everglades in Florida, America, the paperbark tea-tree has spread so widely through the wetlands that it is considered a noxious weed.

Melaleucas grow everywhere in the bush and are widely planted in parks and along streets.

Growing

Melaleucas grow well in poorly-drained, swampy soil and in all but the coldest climates. They tolerate strong winds and salt spray. They will grow on light or clay soils, but are frost-sensitive when young and do best in frost-free places.

The plants are easily propagated from seed or cuttings, grow quickly and, once established, rarely need watering.

Melaleucas make good windbreaks or privacy screens, provide heavy shade and can be cut back heavily to make hedges. There are local species to suit most climates.

Paperbark Wrapups

Peel sheets of paperbark from the melaleuca trunks, wet them and wrap around fish or pieces of meat before baking them in an ordinary oven, barbecue oven, or in hot coals in an outdoor campfire. The paperbark wrapping seals in moisture and spreads its delicate flavour through the food. Whole potatoes can also be cooked this way.

The discarded paperbark sheets make good garden mulch.

PAPERBARK TEA-TREE

Melaleuca quinquenervia (syn. *M. viridiflora*)
Other names: Coastal tea-tree, narrow leaf paperbark

CLIMATE   Frost free, temperate to subtropical
HABITAT   Coastal swamps and lakes from Botany Bay (NSW) to north
           Qld and Papua New Guinea
FORM   Spreading tree, 9–15 m tall, with whitish, thick, papery bark
FOLIAGE   Small, dark green, lemon-scented leaves with longitudinal
           veins and shiny oil glands

FLOWERS   Creamy yellow (sometimes greenish or red) flower spikes, 8–10 cm long, from spring to winter

Growing
Paperbark tea-trees will grow on wet and salty (even brackish) soils and along the coast. They are frost-sensitive.

Tea time
The paperbark tea-tree leaves make an aromatic, lemon-flavoured tea, which is tasty, but not as pleasant as tea made from leptospermum. Aborigines made a sweet drink by steeping dozens of the nectar-laden blossoms in troughs of water. See **Nectar Blossom Cordial, p.105.**

CHAPTER 2

Bushfruits

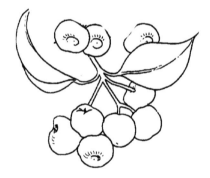

A berry bounty ... The profuse, brightly coloured luscious fruits and berries of the Australian bush and rainforest entice birds, fruit bats and small animals to eat them and disperse their seeds.

We can eat bushfruits raw or cooked in savoury sauces for meat and poultry, or in sweet pies, jams and preserves. The tartness and flavour of most bushfruits goes well with cheese and cheesecake.

APPLEBERRY

Billardiera scandens

Aboriginal names: Bomula, bo-murra cammeral (Eora, Sydney), karrawang (Coranderrk, Vic)

Other names: Apple dumpling, dumpling plant, potato apple, Tasmanian blueberry

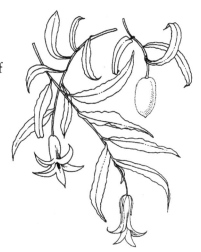

FAMILY	PITTOSPORACEAE
CLIMATE	Temperate
HABITAT	Eucalyptus forests and heaths of E of Australia, from Tas to Qld
FORM	Slender, twining creeper to 3 m, with toothed leaves
FOLIAGE	Furry, wavy-edged, yellow-green leaves to 3 cm long, turn purple as they age
FLOWERS	Creamy or yellow-green tubular flowers, about 2 cm long in spring
FRUITS	Small, elongated yellow or olive-green berries, 2–3 cm long in summer

Appleberries are attractive creepers which in nature twist through trees and shrubs in shady eucalyptus forests to heights of 3 to 6 m. They look spectacular in home gardens, sprawling over fences, trellises and pergolas, or as a matted ground cover which twines around itself.

In spring and summer clusters of bright, graceful tubular flowers hang from the wiry stems like elongated bells. They are followed by small, shiny berries, yellow or olive-green in some species and purple to red in others; they are juicy, with an acid flavour resembling stewed cooking apples.

There are several species, but the best fruits are produced by the widespread common appleberry (*Billardiera scandens*), sweet appleberry (*Billardiera cymosa*) and purple appleberry (*Billardiera longiflora*). In the nineteenth century, children called the plump, sausage-shaped berries 'dumplings'. First Fleet settlers in Port Jackson knew about the Aboriginal use of the species, *Bo-murra cammeral*. Marine Lieutenant William Dawes translated the name to 'the Potatoe apple fruit' in his unpublished notebooks (1790). The species is named after French botanist Jacques de la Labillardiére (1755–1834), who collected plants in Tas in 1792.

Growing
Appleberries are hardy and grow best in full sun or light shade. They prefer warm, well-drained soil, but adapt to sandy or even clay soil if kept well watered. Allow 50 cm between plants.

The plants are propagated from seed or cuttings, but, oddly, the common appleberry is the most difficult to get started, so try to obtain a growing plant from a nursery. Seeds can take 8 to 12 weeks to germinate in spring and autumn. Washing them in detergent may improve germination. Cuttings are difficult to strike.

Once established, young plants grow rapidly and usually fruit in the first year. They can be trained to climb over shrubs.

Each two-celled berry fruit contains numerous seeds, which can be saved by spreading out soft, mature fruits on mesh to dry in the sun, or by fermenting the berries by squashing ripe fruit in a saucer or bowl with a little water and leaving to ferment for a few weeks. When fermentation starts, pour the mass into a strainer and wash off the flesh and retain the seeds. Tomato seeds are treated in much the same way.

Appleberries are good in tubs and hanging baskets. They twine and straggle through other plants without harming them and the lovely green bells attract honeyeaters. You may need tree guards when starting plants in the bush because wallabies like to munch on them.

Eating
Appleberries yield masses of very small fleshy fruits, which weigh about 2 g each. They should not be eaten until thoroughly ripe, are soft and fall from the plants, or start to flush red or purple. The taste is like kiwi fruit and aniseed. The fruits picked green will soften and ripen if you put them in a paper bag with a ripe banana. Add ripe raw appleberries to fruit or berry salads, or cook fruits in muffins, or mix with equal amounts of apples in pies. Fruit freeze well.

RELATED PLANTS
Sweet appleberry (*Billardiera cymosa*)
Sweet appleberry will grow in drier places than common appleberry and germinates readily from fresh seed. Flowers are pink or mauve (about

2 cm in diameter) and bloom in spring and summer. Habitat: NSW, Vic and SA. The green or purple-red berries have an aniseed taste. Shrubs twine and spread to a width of 2 m.

Purple appleberry (*Billardiera longiflora*)
Purple appleberry (or climbing blue berry) thrives in semi-shade and cool, moist conditions.

The climbers have narrow, dark green leaves and pale-green tube flowers in spring and summer, followed by shiny, oval, purple berries which hang from the slender twigs. They have very little flesh and are packed with small seeds. The plant climbs from 2 to 4 m.

Seeds may not germinate until the second year after sowing, but side-shoots strike quickly. Habitat: NSW, Tas, Vic.

> All through the scrubby undergrowth I found the quaint little creeper billardiera — better known to most of us as 'puddings', on account of its fruit, which look like green roly-polies, and have served for many a dinner in our cubby-house days.
>
> Amy E. Mack, *A Bush Calendar* (November), Sydney, 1909

AUSTRAL DOUBAH

Leichhardtia australis (syn. *Marsdenia australis*)
Aboriginal names: Alkwarirra (Utopia, NT), Atnetye (Arrernte, NT), carcular, cogola (Central Australia), endoolah (Gilbert River, Qld), julukgurn (Jawoyn, Katherine, NT), kalkula (Kalgoorlie, WA), mooloory, winejul (Cloncurry River, Qld), untorngo (Anangu, Uluru, NT), jubali yuparli (Walpiri, NT). Pods: Alangwka (Utopia, NT), alangkwe (Arrernte, NT), doobar, doubah, doubar (Central Australia)
Other names: Banana creeper, bush banana, desert banana, native pear

FAMILY	ASCLEPIADACEAE
CLIMATE	Arid, warm, temperate and tropical
HABITAT	Rocky boulders or river beds in the arid, sandy inland
FORM	Small, perennial creeping, twining vines which climb trees and shrubs as high as 2 m
FOLIAGE	Narrow, dull grey-green, pointed leaves, 4–10 cm long,

	covered with greyish hairs. They exude a milky latex if cut or broken
FLOWERS	Small, green-yellow bell-shaped blossoms in clusters
FRUITS	Elongated, tapering, green-fleshed pods, 2–8 cm long, filled with white 'cotton' and black seeds with silky hairs. They appear after rain

Austral doubah, also known as the desert or bush 'banana', does not resemble either native or introduced bananas. Fruits grow on a creeping vine and not a tree; their skin is green, not yellow; and the pods are not shaped like bananas, but look like small, tapering chokos.

The gold mining town of Kalgoorlie (WA) was given the local Aboriginal name for the desert banana.

Growing

Austral doubahs are propagated from seed, which germinates in 2 to 6 weeks. They will also grow from cuttings. Sow seeds directly in the garden in warm weather. Train vines over a trellis, stake, fence or trees.

The vines have adapted well to the Vic mallee.

Eating

Young, green pods—skin, green seeds and pulp—are eaten raw while they are still crunchy, moist and sweet. They have a sticky, milky white sap, but are quite safe to eat. With age, the flesh becomes hard and fibrous and dries out and the pods split to release flattened black, hairy seeds. Older fruits can be baked lightly in hot fire ashes and peeled before eating. When the pods split, the sweet pulp in the centre is easy to pull out whole. Bitter seeds and hairy plumes are discarded.

Desert Aborigines make full use of this versatile plant. They eat the sweet-tasting flowers, young leaves and shoots, roast the tuberous roots (when food is short), and suck nectar from the flowers.

RELATED PLANTS

Magabala (*Marsdenia vividiflora*)
Aboriginal names: Kippli (Gurindji, NT), magabala,
makabala, makapala (Broome, WA)
Other names: Bush banana, green berry creeper, native 'potato'

A tropical twining vine. Fruits are eaten green and immature in the wet
season, when they are crisp and tasty. The leaves, small green flowers and
underground tubers are also eaten.

BURDEKIN PLUM

Pleiogynium timorense (syn. *Pleiogynium cerasiferum; P. solandri;
Spondias pleiogyna*)
Aboriginal names: Bung ya (Bundaberg, Qld), noongi (Port Curtis,
Qld), rancooran (Rockhampton, Qld)
Other names: Sweet plum

FAMILY	ANACARDIACEAE
CLIMATE	Tropical to warm temperate
HABITAT	Rainforest streams and sand dunes of coastal north Qld, Papua New Guinea and Timor
FORM	Shapely, spreading tree, 6–20 m tall, with but tressed trunk
FOLIAGE	Glossy, pinnate leaves, spearshaped, up to 12 cm long, with red- brown new growth
FLOWERS	Small, pale green, densely clustered flowers in summer
FRUITS	Large, purple-black ripe fruits, like flattened plums, 3–5 cm long, contain a woody, ribbed stone

Burdekin plum is an Australian relative of the cashew nut (*Anarcardium
occidentale*) and the mango (*Magnifera indica*).

Growing

The trees are hardy, tolerate some frost and withstand dry spells. They grow well in fertile, well-drained soil with plenty of moisture, but will adapt to sandy soil. Propagate from seed or cuttings. Seeds are slow to germinate. Plant in an open, sunny spot, spacing trees 10 to 12 m apart.

Burdekin plums grow widely throughout Qld (including Brisbane) and fruit well as far south as Sydney's North shore.

Eating

At the Endeavour River (near Townsville, Qld) in June 1779, Joseph Banks noted in his journal: 'Another fruit about as large as a small golden pippin but flatter, of a deep purple colour; these when gathered off from the tree were very hard and disagreeable but after being kept a few days became soft and tasted much like indifferent damsons [plums].'

The thin layer of flesh around the pumpkin-like stone is more palatable when overripe or 'bletted' like European medlars. Aborigines softened the fruits by burying them in sand for up to two weeks after picking. They also ate the fruits dried.

Burdekin plums are used for making jam, but the fruit contains no pectin, so it will not 'gel' unless pectin is added (see **Bushfruit jam**, p.32). Try the juiced fruits as a cordial syrup, diluted with water.

CHERRY BALLART

Exocarpus cupressformis
Aboriginal names: Ballee (Yarra, Vic),
balle, ballat (Gippsland, Vic), ballot,
palatt (Lake Condah, Vic), ko-ie-yatt
(NSW), tchimmi-dillen (Qld)
Other names: Native or wild cherry

FAMILY	SANTALACEAE
CLIMATE	Temperate
HABITAT	Widespread through euca lypt forests of SE Australia
FORM	Small tree, shaped like a weeping cypress, reaches 2–7 m
FOLIAGE	Thin, soft, drooping, light green, 'leafless' branches

FLOWERS   Minute green-yellow flowers, summer to winter
FRUITS   Each small, true fruit or seed is attached to a long, fleshy
           flower stalk, which is green at first, then scarlet or orange
           when swollen and ripe in winter and spring

The cherry ballart is a curious and intriguing plant. The hard seed or true fruit is on the 'outside', like a cashew nut, and is supported on a large, succulent stalk which looks like the fruit and is the part that is eaten.

The fruits were likened to a European cherry with the stone outside by British botanists, who cited it as yet another example of the way Nature was reversed in the Southern hemisphere when compared with the Northern hemisphere. The Yarra Aborigines in Vic used the close-grained wood for making spear throwers.

RELATED PLANTS
Alpine ballart (*Exocarpus nanus*)
A cool temperate dwarf shrub, otherwise similar to cherry ballart.

Broad-leaved native cherry (*Exocarpus latifolius*)
Also called scrub sandalwood.

Subtropical to tropical shrub, found in rainforests and on the coast from northern NSW to Cape York and the NT. Fruit are yellow.

Broom ballart (*Exocarpus sparteus*)
Aboriginal name: Djuk (Nyunga, WA)
Upright yellow-green shrub to 3.5 m, found in all states except Tas. Fruits are very small, but borne profusely (November to January in the Perth area). To collect the fruit, the Nyunga spread kangaroo skins under the bushes and shook them. Fruit are sweeter after turning from orange-brown to crimson.

Pale-fruit ballart (*Exocarpus strictus*)
Also called pearl ballart.

Small, erect trees bear pearly white fruit stalks and black fruits. Habitat: Temperate forests of Tas, Vic and NSW.

Growing
Cherry ballarts are root parasites like the related quandong (*Santalum accuminatum*). Plants grow normally from seed and then the roots intercept

those of nearby plants and tap into their water and nutrient supply.

Plant seedlings near a native grass which will act as a host. As plants mature, they are able to obtain some nutrients for themselves. The seeds and cuttings are difficult to propagate. The seeds germinate more readily when they have been digested and voided by birds.

There are cherry ballart species for every kind of climate.

Eating

The 'fruits'—really the stalks—of cherry ballart are fleshy, sweet and palatable and were eaten raw by Aborigines and colonial settlers, especially children. They make good thirst quenchers on a hot day. Discard the green seed or 'pip' at the tip.

DAVIDSON'S PLUM

Davidsonia pruriens
Aboriginal name: Orray (Qld)
Other names: Sour plum

FAMILY	DAVIDSONIACEAE
CLIMATE	Warm temperate to subtropical
HABITAT	Rainforests from northern NSW to N Qld, from sea-level to 1000 m
FORM	Tall, thin, palm-like tree, often with many trunks, 4–6 m high, spreading 2–4 m in cultivation
FOLIAGE	Large, toothed leaves, 6–30 cm long, with pink tips, are covered in rusty, irritating hairs
FLOWERS	Tiny mauve or pink flowers in long racemes
FRUITS	Plum-sized purple fruits with scarlet flesh hang in clusters on the trunk, to 5 cm long, ripen both summer and autumn

Davidson's plum has been cultivated for over a century. In 1898, Mr A. J. Hockings had been growing a specimen tree in his South Brisbane garden for many years. Queensland's Colonial Botanist, Mr F. Manson Bailey, believed that by careful selection and cultivation Davidson's plum 'might become a valuable addition to our cultivated kinds [of fruit]'.

In *Wild Food in Australia* (1974), botanists Alan and Joan Cribb rated Davidson's plum as 'one of the best native fruits we know' and Tim Low, in

Bush Tucker (1989), called it the 'queen of Australian rainforest "plums"'. Wild food foragers generally agree that Davidson's plums make the best Australian bush jam and wine. Trees are now rare in nature, except in wet rainforests, but are sold by many nurseries as ornamental plants.

The trees bear prolific amounts of furry fruit which has reddish flesh like the European plum. Fruit begin to drop from the tree when they are ripe, soft and juicy.

Growing

Davidson's plum prefers warm conditions, but will tolerate cooler temperatures in places with only occasional light frosts. Propagate from the small, flattened seeds or from cuttings. Fresh seeds from the fruit flesh planted in summer will germinate in a few weeks.

Plant in semi-shade, preferably under taller trees, sheltered from strong or dry winds. Trees do best in fertile soil and given plenty of humus and regular watering. The seedling trees make good pot plants for courtyards, small gardens and indoors.

Eating

'This plum, which is in perfection about July, is largely used by settlers for making into jam and jelly, as well as an addition to pie-melon or pumpkin [in jam], to which it imparts an agreeable acid and rich colouring' wrote F. M. Bailey.

Scrub fruits lightly to remove the hairs, then wash well. Wear gloves, because you might have an allergic reaction to the hairs. The fruits are very acid and sour if eaten fresh, but the juice is excellent in salad dressings in place of vinegar. They are delicious stewed with sugar or honey, or made into dark red jam, jelly or wine. Try them with roast duck instead of sour cherries. The fruit can be frozen, bottled or cooked as a preserve.

RELATED PLANTS

Smooth Davidson's plum (*Davidsonia pruriens* var. *jerseyana*)

This form is now rare in the wild and considered to be an endangered species. However, there are 36 robust trees growing in the bushfruit garden at the House With No Steps at Alstonville (NSW).

The trees bear smooth-skinned fruit and smaller, hairless leaves than the common Davidson's plum. Fruit are 3 to 6 cm in diameter. Their dark purple, soft, juicy pulp can be made into jam or jelly.

The seed is sterile and plants will only grow from cuttings, but will bear heavily in humid conditions. Multi-trunked trees may grow to 15 m.

Bushfruit Jam

The pectin levels in fruit determine the setting quality of jam made from them. If pectin levels are low, or you don't know what the level is, add lemon or orange juice, which are very high in pectin.

Pectin is commercially available, but you can usually make do without it.

A very rough guide to jam making is: 1 kg of fruit to 1 kg of sugar.

2 kg bushfruit, washed, peeled and seeded if necessary
2 litres water
2 kg caster sugar
juice of 2 or 3 lemons/oranges

Cut fruit into smallish pieces. Boil in the water, with the juice, for about 20 minutes, or until the fruit is tender.

Mix in the sugar and continue to boil gently, stirring often, until the jam is the required consistency. Bottle and seal in sterilised jars.

Test: to see if jam is done, drop a small amount onto a cold plate and let it cool. It should shrivel up when pushed by a spoon.

Feasting on figs

Wild figs grow throughout the warmer parts of mainland Australia.

Aborigines eat some kinds of figs raw; others they pound into a cake or smooth paste, or soak in water to which they add 'sugarbag' honey collected from native bees.

Make sure figs are completely ripe and soft before you eat them fresh.

Native figs have smooth bark and a milky sap and are fertilised by wasps.

ROCK FIG
Ficus platypoda
Aboriginal names: Ili, ilyi (Anangu, Uluru, NT), nyuta (Turrubul, Brisbane), wijirrki (Warlpiri, NT)
Other names: Desert fig, native fig, small fig, wild fig

FAMILY	MORACEAE
CLIMATE	Arid to warm temperate
HABITAT	Rocky hills, ledges and rock faces in gorges near inland waterholes
FORM	Much-branched, twisting, spreading shrub to 4 m, spreading to 6 m
FOLIAGE	Smooth, glossy, oval, pointed, dark green leaves, 4–19 cm long, with prominent midribs
FLOWERS	Small white-yellow flowers, in spring, or after rain
FRUITS	Many small yellow-green fruits, which turn black-red when ripe, depending on rainfall

In 1874 the explorer John Forrest often found rock figs during his journey through desert country from WA to the Overland Telegraph line in Central Australia. Wild rock figs grew abundantly near the cave where gold prospector Harold Lasseter sheltered at Lake Christopher, west of Lake Amadeus, NT in 1931.

In Central Australia, rock figs climb the steep faces at the base of Uluru (Ayers Rock) and nearby Kata Tjuta (the Olgas).

Growing

In nature, rock figs push their roots through rock crevices and spread their low branches at ground level or climb up the face of cliffs. They are ideal for a rockery or rocky garden site. Plant in pockets of fertile soil.

Eating

Rock figs are sweet and juicy when eaten fresh and ripe, straight from the tree. Large trees are prolific, often bearing thousands of fruit. The small, olive-sized figs taste like European figs and make good preserves.

RELATED PLANTS

A hairy-leaved rock fig (*Ficus platypoda* var. *lachocaulon*) is native to NW Australia.

PORT JACKSON FIG

Ficus rubignosa
Aboriginal names: Dthaaman, tam-mun (Eora, Sydney),
dthaman (Dharug, Camden, NSW)
Other names: Rusty fig

FAMILY	MORACEAE
CLIMATE	Temperate to subtropical
HABITAT	Coast and ranges from Bateman's Bay (NSW) to southern Qld
FORM	A climber, smaller and with a smoother, unbuttressed trunk than the Moreton Bay fig, reaching 4–10 m in height
FOLIAGE	Elliptical thick leaves to 10 cm, shiny, with rusty coloured hairs on the underside
FLOWERS	Small, yellow
FRUITS	In pairs, about 1 cm in diameter, ripening summer and autumn

The Eora Aboriginal people around Sydney Harbour ate the small yellow fruits of the Port Jackson fig raw or preserved in a 'cake'. While tracing the Parramatta River in 1788, Governor Arthur Phillip did not see any Aborigines, but found a half eaten cake made from crushed figs.

In February 1790, Marine Lieutenant Ralph Clark went ashore at Sydney Harbour 'at a fig tree of which we ate a great many all of us in the boat, they being ripe but before we got home they all gave us the grips [gripes]'.

Writing in 1811, David Dickinson Mann described the Sydney wild figs as 'nauseous, full of seed, but eaten by the natives'. Aborigines continued to value the Port Jackson fig a century after white settlement. 'Wherever you may see one of the fig-trees growing, so surely you will find a blackfellow's camp or home alongside,' wrote James S. Bray in a report on a burial ground at Middle Harbour in 1888.

Growing

The trees are best propagated from cuttings.

The Port Jackson fig starts life as an epiphyte, a seedling growing in the fork of a tree or in crevices on sandstone cliffs, which in time are covered by its tangled roots. There are ancient specimens on the Tarpeian cliff, near the Sydney Opera House.

These trees are too big for most suburban gardens. They are more cold tolerant than Moreton Bay or sandpaper fig and tolerate salt spray, though it may stunt their growth.

Eating
Fruits are small, but very tasty and should only be eaten fresh when they are completely ripe, soft and pulpy.

RELATED PLANTS
Moreton Bay Fig (*Ficus macrophylla*)
Aboriginal names: Budheh (Bundjalung, northern NSW), ngoa-nga (Turrubul, Brisbane), gunnin (Noonuccal, Moreton Bay, Qld), kar-reuaira (Dharug, Camden, NSW)

The well-known Moreton Bay figs are giant spreading trees, reaching 18 to 25 or even 50 m in height, too big for most home gardens. There are some notable specimens, like the huge old trees at Fig Tree Cottage, Hunters Hill (Sydney) and others at Aberglasslyn House, Maitland, NSW.

It is an excellent tree for shade and shelter on the farm, but their invasive spreading roots make Moreton Bay figs unsuitable for home gardens or orchards. Cattle eat the figs and foliage.

The trees grow in temperate to subtropical climates, from Illawarra, NSW, to north Qld and require 1000 to 2150 cm (40 to 60 inches) of rain annually. The large, yellow-fleshed figs are not as good to eat fresh as other native figs, but can be cooked in tarts or made into jam.

CREEK SANDPAPER FIG
Ficus opposita
Aboriginal names: Punjarri (Gurinji, NT), ulowang (Dharug, Camden, NSW), yuk kom (Wik, NT)
Other names: Creek fig, mountain fig, rough-leaved fig, sandpaper fig

FAMILY	MORACEAE
CLIMATE	Subtropical
HABITAT	Creek banks of coastal rainforests, from eastern Vic to Mackay (Qld) and NT

FORM	Deciduous tree, 12–16 m
FLOWERS	Small, creamy white
FOLIAGE	The rough, dark green leaves, covered with stiff, spiny hairs, drop in spring and regrow in summer
FRUITS	Marble-sized round fruit in clusters, red-purple or red-brown when ripe

In August 1770 Joseph Banks noted that the Aborigines at the Endeavour River (Qld) polished their spears using the rough leaves of the sandpaper fig like a rasp. Its leaf, wrote Banks, 'bites upon wood almost as keenly as our European shave grass used by the Joiners'.

Manmagun tyibung wellan madwara
We will gather tyibungs [geebungs] *as we come back*

Sometime in 1791, on the shores of Sydney Cove, Marine Lieutenant William Dawes took up pen and ink and wrote down these words in the language of the Eora people of the Sydney area, and in English. The words resonate across space and time between two cultures.

The small notebook in which Dawes recorded Eora words and phrases, titled *Vocabulary of N.S. Wales in the neighbourhood of Sydney (Native and English)*, is held in the Marsden Collection of the School of Oriental and African Studies at London University.

From information gathered from his Eora informants, Dawes concluded that the Sydney Aborigines separated food-bearing plants into three main kinds — *wigi* or wild berries and fruits (including the geebung), nectar-bearing blossom plants such as banksias, melaleucas and waratahs, and tuberous rooted plants, like yams, which grew along the Hawkesbury River.

Growing

Sandpaper figs are suited to large suburban gardens. The fruit are borne on old growth after the large leaves are shed.

Eating

One of the most delicious native figs, sweet when fully ripe, especially in good seasons. Peel off the hairy skin before eating the pulpy seed mass.

RELATED PLANTS

Another sandpaper fig (*Ficus coronata*) reaches 15 m.

A tropical fig (*Ficus racemosa*), which bears its fruits on little knobbly stems on old branches, grows at the water's edge in Arnhemland, NT. Fruits are eaten raw when ripe and red. They also grow further inland and are eaten by the Gurinji people.

GEEBUNG
FAMILY PROTEACEAE
Aboriginal names: Babadul, babathool (Gundungurra, Blue Mountains, NSW), dulandella (Turrubul, Brisbane), tyibung (Eora, Sydney), jibong, jibbong (NSW)

For the Australian Aborigines, the fruits of the geebung must have been the original bush snack. Though the flesh is meagre and astringent, it is succulent, and makes a good thirst quencher.

There are many species of geebungs growing throughout Australia, from cool temperate to tropical areas. Of the 75 Australian species, about 28 are found in SW WA. There is one New Zealand species.

The genus was named by Edward Smith in 1798 after the South African born mycologist, Christiaan Hendrick Persoon (1755–1836).

Geebungs are shrubs or small trees, with brown, papery trunks. To prevent excess evaporation in dry weather, the plants are able to twist their leaves sideways, so that full sunlight does not fall on the broad part of the leaf.

In spring and summer they bear small, bell-shaped, cream to yellow tubular flowers, so pretty that they are now being cultivated for the cut-flower industry.

Geebung fruits, like peaches and plums, are drupes, soft and fleshy on the outside, with a woody stone, containing one or two seeds. Unlike plums or peaches, there is only a thin layer of flesh around the stone. The fruit are of various sizes, in large clusters that weigh down the branches, though at other times they may be large and grow separately. They are in season from early spring throughout summer. They fall when they are ripe.

Writing in 1893, David Crichton said the bright green foliage of geebungs was used in Sydney to make decorative wreaths 'as the leaves retain their rigidity longer than most other evergreen shrubs'. Geebung, although an Eora (Sydney) word, gave its name to the Brisbane suburb.

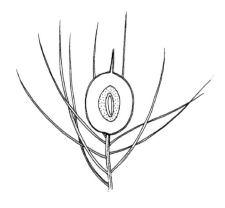

Growing

Although common in the bush, geebungs are difficult plants to propagate. If conditions are right, cuttings of ripened wood of the current season will strike in sand in a pot under glass or a plastic bag. Treating cuttings with hormone powder assists propagation. Layering is another possible method.

Early growth is slow, but once established, plants are hardy. They thrive in peaty as well as well-drained soils.

When young growth is yellow, with darker green veins, there could be an iron deficiency, which can be treated by adding iron chelates to the soil.

Eating

Raw geebung fruits should be very ripe and soft before you eat them and taste better if the skin is removed. Unripe fruit is stringy or like cotton wool. Don't eat the seeds.

Fruits have a high vitamin C content.

A good way to preserve a quantity of geebungs is to make the pulp into fruit leather.

BROAD-LEAVED GEEBUNG

Persoonia levis (syn. *Persoonia laevis*; *P. salacina*)
Other names: Paperbark, smooth, or willow geebung

CLIMATE	Cool to warm temperate
HABITAT	Heath and open forest through Vic to northern NSW
FORM	Shrub, 1–5 m high with curved branches and loose, flaky, papery red-black bark
FOLIAGE	Bright green, broad, sickle-shaped, thick, leathery, veined leaves, 5–20 cm long
FLOWERS	Yellow tubular flowers, 1 cm long, at end of branches in summer
FRUITS	Stringy, succulent fruit, 5 mm in diameter, with a spike or style

The broad-leaved geebung is a small shrub, only 1 m in height, with shorter, broad, rounded leaves. It tolerates mild frosts and some salt, and grows well on open heaths.

RELATED PLANTS
Another broad-leaved geebung (*Persoonia corrifolia*) grows in the sandy soil around Brisbane.

NARROW-LEAVED GEEBUNG
Persoonia linearis
Aboriginal name: Naam-burra (Illawarra, NSW)

CLIMATE	Temperate to subtropical
HABITAT	Understorey forest shrub through Vic, NSW and Qld
FORM	Open, spreading shrub to 3 m high and broad with dark, flaky, papery bark
FOLIAGE	Narrow, straight, dull, dark green leaves, 4–6 cm long, on drooping branches
FLOWERS	Yellow flowers, summer to winter
FRUITS	Fruit are ripe when green

PINE-LEAVED GEEBUNG
Persoonia pinnifolia

CLIMATE	Temperate
HABITAT	Open forests and sandstone ridges of NSW
FORM	Bushy, spreading shrub, 2–4 m high
FOLIAGE	Crowded, fine, soft, light-green leaves like pine needles
FLOWERS	Clusters of hanging, scented yellow flowers in spikes, summer to autumn
FRUITS	Succulent fruits, ripening from green to bronze-purple, hang in bunches like grapes

The pine-leaved geebung is native to NSW and can be seen growing in the Royal National Park, south of Sydney. This species is used for cut flowers because it flowers for up to six months.

An attractive shrub, with handsome drooping foliage which bends under the weight of the fruit clusters. They are hardy and grow quickly to full size, but require watering in summer.

Seeds are spread widely by feasting birds (including emus).

RELATED PLANTS

Tasmanian geebung (*Persoonia gunni*)
Also called Gunn's geebung.

Cool temperate shrub, 1.5 to 2 m high. Fruits are green with a purple flush and follow clusters of creamy white perfumed summer flowers.

Prickly geebung (*Persoonia juniperina*)
A cool to temperate climate prickly bush, 60 cm to 1 m tall, bearing yellow flowers in summer, followed by green fruits. Drought tolerant.

SICKLE-LEAVED GEEBUNG

Persoonia falcata
Aboriginal names: Booral (Mitchell River, Qld),
nanchee (Kimberleys, WA and Mitchell River, Qld),
wankid (Nyul Nyul, Broome area, WA)
Other names: Sickle-leaved milky plum

CLIMATE	Tropical
HABITAT	Open forest, sandy soil or swamps from north Qld to Broome (WA)
FORM	Upright shrub
FOLIAGE	Long, narrow, sickle-shaped leaves
FLOWERS	Bright yellow tubular flowers in spikes at twig ends, in spring
FRUITS	Small, smooth-skinned, green-yellow fruit when ripe in the wet season (summer)

SNOTTYGOBBLE

Persoonia longifolia (syn. *Persoonia elliptica*)
Other names: Snotty bobs, wild pear

CLIMATE	Temperate
HABITAT	Jarrah forests of SW Australia, from Perth to Albany (WA)
FORM	Low, scrubby bush, 1–1.5 m high
FOLIAGE	Narrow, needle-like leaves, 4–10 cm long
FLOWERS	Yellow cylindrical flowers, about 1 cm long, winter to summer
FRUITS	Fleshy, pear-shaped fruits ripen Oct–Nov

This geebung really is called the snottygobble plant in WA! We thought at first that this might have something to do with the little protruding spiky 'nose' at the end of each green fruit. However, it seems that the name refers to the mucus-like gelatinous matter surrounding the seed when ripe fruits split open.

Snottygobbles were a staple food, eaten for their moisture and succulence by the Nyungar people of SW Australia. Ripe fruits fall to the ground if the bush is shaken. Plants grow in sandy, gravelly soil.

RELATED PLANTS

Pouched snottygobble (*Persoonia saccata*)
Aboriginal names: Cadgeegurrup (Nyunga, WA)
This geebung has a 'pouch' on the lower side of each flower. It grows widely through sandy woodlands in WA.

Another snottygobble, *Persoonia elliptica*, has elliptical leaves.

ILLAWARRA PLUM

Podocarpus elatus
Aboriginal names: Daalgaal (Barron River, Qld), gidneywallum (Gubbi Gubbi, Qld)
Other names: Brown pine, plum pine

FAMILY	PODOCARPACEAE
CLIMATE	Subtropical to cool temperate
HABITAT	Rainforest conifer, E coast from Bateman's Bay (NSW) to Cairns (Qld)
FORM	Large, upright evergreen tree, 5–20 m tall, with spreading crown

FOLIAGE	Stiff, dark green, glossy, narrow, oblong, sharp-pointed leaves, 5–17 cm long
FLOWERS	Flowers on male and female trees
FRUITS	Masses of vivid purple, fleshy, plum-like fruits, 2–3 cm in diameter, early autumn to winter

The Illawarra plum or plum pine has sweet flesh and can be eaten raw. It is destined to become a bushfruit star. It is a pine tree which has no cones and which bears fruits which are not at all like plums.

The trees were cut down for timber and are no longer common in the wild, but many have been planted by councils as park, garden and street trees as far south as Melbourne.

In 1998 some 500 trees were planted commercially. Steven Pashley, executive chef of Brisbane's Gazebo Hotel, and his wife Leonie have planted Illawarra plums, riberries and lemon myrtle in their bushfood plantation west of Brisbane.

Growing

Illawarra plums adapt to a wide range of climates and withstand heavy frosts. Trees grow well in Sydney, Melbourne and Canberra.

The edible dark purple fruit is a swollen stem of the female tree. The external seed, which is not edible, sits in a hard shell protruding from the fruit. Male trees are needed for fertilisation, one male for several female fruit-bearing trees.

Seedling rootstocks are strong. Propagation from seed is slow and unreliable. Try cuttings.

The trees are slow growing when young, taking one year to establish roots and a further year to settle in, but are long-lived. Most soils and aspects are suitable, but they grow and yield sooner in fertile soil.

Eating

The fruits of the Illawarra plum are sweet, with a plum-pine or 'pine wine' flavour. When fully ripe, they fall from the tree, and can be eaten fresh. Some people say the taste improves if you leave them in the refrigerator overnight to allow the sugars to develop. The fruits have a high vitamin C content (10 to 11 per cent).

Illawarra plums have a gummy texture due to the resinous central core, and this makes them unsuitable for boiling into a compote. They can be gently simmered for jam or for tart or pie fillings. Fruit can be frozen for later use. When making jam or cooking the fruit, discard the central core and its pips.

Whole fruits can be made into chutneys and sauces for barbecues. They are popular in bushfood restaurants.

RELATED PLANTS

Brown pine (*Podocarpus dispersus*)
A large, straight rainforest tree to 20 m, bearing fruit with edible red flesh and native to the Atherton Tableland (north Qld).

Mountain plum pine (*Podocarpus lawrencei*; syn. *Podocarpus alpina*)
A dwarf alpine version of the Illawarra plum, spreads gnarled branches over rocks, but a tree will grow to 2 to 3 m tall in mountain forests, and bear hard small fruits. Native to Vic and Tas. Slow growing, but can withstand snow.

KAKADU PLUM

Terminalia ferdinandiana
Deciduous
Aboriginal names: Gabiny, gubiny, kabiny (Broome-Derby, WA), marlak, warawitj (Jawoyn, Katherine, NT), murrgin (Jirrbal, Qld), murunga (eastern Arnhemland, NT)
Other names: Arnhemland, billygoat, green or wild plum

FAMILY	COMBRETACEAE
CLIMATE	Subtropical to tropical
HABITAT	Behind coastal sand dunes of NW Australia
FORM	Tall, slender tree to 10 m
FOLIAGE	Light green-yellow leaves which drop in spring
FLOWERS	Creamy flower spikes in early summer
FRUITS	Olive-sized light green waxy fruit with thin skin and one stone, yellow or purple when ripe in autumn to winter in Arnhem Land, NT, and in the wet season around Broome, WA.

Kakadu plum, coined by television's Bush Tucker Man, Major Les Hiddins, has become the marketing name for the former green, wild, or billygoat plum (fruit were said to have a 'goat-like' face). It has the highest content of vitamin C of any fruit in the world.

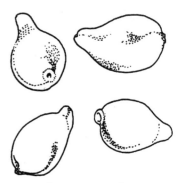

As a result of fieldwork by Hiddens and bush tucker pioneer Vic Cherikoff, kakadu plums were analysed by the Human Nutrition Unit at the University of Sydney and found to contain more than 50 times more ascorbic acid (vitamin C) than citrus fruits.

The oval green fruits, which resemble olives or geebungs, are about 2 cm long and 1 cm in diameter and contain a large stone. Kakadu plums are related to the Indian almond (*Terminalia cattapa*).

Growing
Kakadu plums grow in sandy loam in warm, moist conditions. They require full sun, high rainfall in summer, and a dry winter. A fine shade tree. Plants are killed by frost and will not grow in cold places.

The seeds germinate in 6 to 12 weeks. To accelerate germination, remove the fleshy layer and scratch the seed case (as with wattle seed). Fruit grows in clusters along the branches.

Eating
Kakadu plums can be eaten raw, or made into sauce, jam or chutney. Because of their high acid content they pickle well. They are ripe when they soften and turn from pale green to yellow or purple. It is difficult to remove the flesh from the stone. They have a sour taste, rather like English gooseberries, even after cooking. The taste is not improved by stewing and fruit do not freeze well. Ice cream flavoured with ripples of kakadu plum is now on sale at supermarkets.

In the NT, Kakadu plums are eaten by Aboriginal children as a snack to quench thirst in the same way as the geebung is used in southern Australia. A drink can be made by pounding the ripe fruit, soaking it in water and adding sugar.

RELATED PLANTS
Nut tree (*Terminalia arostrata*)
The seed or nut can be eaten after it is extracted it from the fruit. It is about the same size as a peanut and has a similar taste. Tropical habitat.

Wild peach (*Terminalia carpentariae*)
Aboriginal name: Mardunggudj (Ramingining, NT)

Green ripe fruits look and taste like dried peaches and can be eaten raw. Large trees grow in the tropical NT.

Native almond (*Terminalia grandiflora*)
The flowers grow in small white clusters like a white bottlebrush. The nuts have a large, pointed, thick, woody shell. From May to October you can crack them between two stones to obtain the edible kernels.

Habitat: Open forests and sandy soil of the Top End and Groote Eylandt.

LEMON ASPEN
Acronychia acidula

FAMILY	RUTACEAE
CLIMATE	Tropical to temperate
HABITAT	Highland rainforests, from central to north Qld
FORM	Umbrella-shaped tree, 10–20 m tall
FOLIAGE	Large, glossy, elliptical dark green leaves, 7–26 cm long, with a spicy aroma when crushed
FLOWERS	Small, creamy, four-petalled showy, scented flowers in dense clusters, in autumn
FRUITS	Lemon or cream, scented, wrinkled, globular, four-segmented fruit, 2–3 cm in diameter, in bunches, autumn to winter

Growing
Lemon aspen adapts to cooler climates where there is good rainfall and rich, fertile soil. Trees are fast-growing if watered well. They are found planted in parks. Germination is very slow, even from fresh seed. It is quicker if the black seeds are removed from the fruit pulp before sowing, but may still take from six weeks to six months or more.

Cuttings root easily and can be planted in full sun or semi-shade.

Eating
Lemon aspen fruits are crisp and aromatic, with a strong flavour when raw. The tiny, crunchy black seeds are edible.

These fruits come into their own in desserts. Lemon is a favourite flavour for ice cream, steamed puddings and tarts. They hold their shape well when gently stewed with sugar, which makes them ideal for glacé fruits, compote or for making jam or marmalade.

Juiced fruit tastes like grapefruit and is good in salad dressings.

RELATED PLANTS

Fuzzy aspen (*Acronychia vestita*)
Similar to lemon aspen, with hairy leaves and wrinkled yellow fruits.

Netted yellow wood (*Acronychia bauerlenii*)
A smaller tree (to 9 m), which bears larger, aromatic fruits and inner bark and has leaves with netted veins.
Habitat: Vic, NSW, Qld.

Yellow wood (*Acronychia oblonquifolia*)
Bears cream-green flowers and globular, succulent, but very acid fruits.
Habitat: The sheltered streams of Qld, NSW and Vic.

Glacé Bushfruits

1 kg bushfruits, fresh or frozen
500 ml water
caster sugar

Bring bushfruits to the boil in cold water and boil for 5 minutes.

Strain fruit and place in a clean container. Boil the liquid with one cup of sugar and pour over the fruit. Leave overnight.

Strain and repeat the process, adding another cup of sugar to the liquid. Repeat this daily. The more often this is done, the thicker the syrup becomes. You must do this seven to 10 times at least!

Use the glacé fruit in cakes or desserts and as the syrup in cordials. Eventually, the fruit may be dried and crystallised.

Fruits to glacé

Lemon aspen, Quandongs, Riberries

LILLY PILLIES

Acmena and *Syzigium* (formerly *Eugenia*) species
FAMILY MYRTACEAE
Evergreen

The name lilly pilly used to apply only to one species, *Acmena smithii*, but now refers to all the related plants. Botanists have split the species into *Acmena* and *Syzigium* from the former *Eugenia* (named after Prince Eugene of Saxony).

There are some 52 species of lilly pilly in Australia, all with edible fruit. Some species are confined to wet rainforests in the far north, and closely related plants are staple foods in Indonesia and South America.

Lilly pillies yield masses of fruit which can be added to fruit salads or made into jams and jelly, fragrant sauces and preserves.

They were among the first native fruits that the settlers ate. While Joseph Banks spent the day (3 May 1770) drying plants on paper (said to be loose pages from Milton's *Paradise Lost*) on a sail in the sun at Botany Bay, James Cook and the botanist Daniel Solander were out in a small boat collecting plants. They found '… several trees which bore fruit of the Jambosa … kind,' Banks wrote in his journal, 'much in colour and shape resembling cherries; of these they eat plentifully and brought home also abundance, which we eat with much pleasure tho they had little to recommend them but a slight acid.'

Growing

Cultivated lilly pilly trees are widely planted as shade trees in parks and gardens, where they grow to about 12 m in height. Wild trees reach 20 to 30 m. Miniature lilly pillies are now being promoted as an attractive low hedge or tub plant, which can be shaped like topiary trees. They are widely available in plant nurseries. They are pretty trees, especially when new young growth colours the leaves bright shades of pink and red. We have a compact 'select' form of bush cherry (*Syzigium australe*), only 45 cm in height, thriving in a pot in our courtyard.

They are easily propagated from seed, grow best on moist, well-composted soil and need ample watering. Lilly pillies grow along creek banks and other watercourses. Make sure they are planted well away from drains and sewers, or they could cause problems. Trees may not bear fruit every year, but some years bear prolifically.

Eating

Lilly pillies may be eaten raw when ripe, but the consensus is that the taste is too acidic. Ripe fruits, which contain large amounts of vitamin C, are best made into juice, jelly or jam. Discard the seeds.

PURPLE LILLY PILLY

Acmena smithii (syn. *Eugenia smithii*)
Aboriginal names: Coochin-coochin (Qld), tdjerail (Illawarra, NSW)
Other names: Creek lilly pilly, satinash, southern lilly pilly

CLIMATE	Temperate to tropical
HABITAT	Coastal rain forests of eastern Australia, from Wilson's Promontory (Vic) to Cape York (Qld)
FORM	Shapely, upright tree, reaching 3–6 m (taller in the wild)
FOLIAGE	Glossy, dark green leaves, 10 cm long
FLOWERS	Small, fluffy, cream-green in clusters, in summer, for up to 3 months
FRUITS	Round, purple, white with a purple tinge, or pink berries, 1 cm in diameter, ripen profusely, winter to summer. The best known and most widely planted lilly pilly apart from the riberry.

Growing

The trees are hardy, but frost tender when young, and prone to attack by scale insects in the cooler southern states. They are fire-resistant, salt-tolerant and adapt to a variety of soils, from wet to dry. The plants strike readily from tip cuttings and can be trimmed to make a hedge 1 m tall. Dwarf forms are now available as well as varieties with variegated leaves. The narrow-leaved 'Mini pilly' grows to the size of a small shrub.

Eating

The acid fruit of purple lilly pilly is refreshing to eat raw when fresh, but there is not much flesh and many people think that the taste has been overrated.

RELATED PLANTS

Blue lilly pilly (*Syzigium oleosumi*; syn. *Eugenia coolminianum*; *E. cyanocarpa*)

Other names: Blue cherry, oily satinash

A small, bushy tree, reaching 3 to 10 m and spreading 3 to 5 m, with white, fluffy, aromatic flowers, and rounded, pale pink fruits, 2.5 cm in diameter, which turn purple when ripe, from autumn to winter. Raw fruit are crisp and juicy, but sometimes resinous.

The small, loose, single globe-shaped seed can rattle in the central cavity when the fruit is ripe. Suited to courtyard tubs. Habitat: Temperate to tropical rainforests from NSW to Cape York (Qld).

BRUSH CHERRY

Syzigium australe (previously *Syzigium paniculatum*)
Aboriginal names: Galang-arra (Dharug, Camden, NSW)
Other names: Brush cherry, creek satinash, scrub cherry

CLIMATE	Subtropical to temperate
HABITAT	Rainforests, along creeks, from Nowra (NSW) to Mossman (Qld)
FORM	Bushy shrub or tree, 3–5 m high and 2–3 m wide
FOLIAGE	Dense, glossy, thick, dark green leaves, 3–10 cm long, with visible oil dots
FLOWERS	Fluffy white, in summer
FRUIT	Small pink to red oval berries (like riberries), 1–2 cm long, borne singly or in bunches, all year

Growing

Propagate by seeds. They resemble eucalyptus seeds.

Brush cherries are hardy and grow well in home gardens and in sandy soils in a wide range of climates. Trees will grow in full sun or semi-shade, but not in arid areas, although they do well around Gawler, SA, which can be quite dry. They are moderately frost and damp-hardy and succeed on the coast. Plants need similar care to the purple lilly pilly.

Eating

Brush cherry fruit are succulent, with a more tangy flavour than the purple lilly pilly. Aborigines ate the fruit raw, but settlers made it into jam and wine.

Bushfruit Cordial

Any bushfruits can be made into cordial or thick fruit 'juice'. It's not necessary to take out the pits or stones.

Use ripe, well-washed fruit.

Cover with water. Add sugar or honey to taste.

Bring to the boil and simmer for at least 20 minutes. The more water boils away the thicker the resulting cordial. Strain well.

Use as a drink base with water or mineral water, or to make jelly. If thick enough use as a sauce over ice cream.

Bottled, this cordial will keep for some time in the refrigerator.

Aussie-style Jelly

4 cups diluted bushfruit cordial, or 1 cup of diced bushfruits cooked in 3 to 4 cups of water or apple juice

1 ½ tablespoons powdered agar agar

Splash of port or brandy (optional)

Sprinkle of powdered lemon myrtle or other spice

Honey, sugar, maple syrup or cider gum sap to taste (probably not necessary if using bushfruit cordial)

Put cordial or cooked bushfruits and liquid into a saucepan over a high heat. When nearly boiling, sprinkle on the agar agar powder, stirring constantly and allow to boil for about 2 minutes.

Remove from heat. Stir in the rest of the ingredients and pour into a wet mould, bowl, or individual dishes.

Allow to cool and refrigerate until set.

Easy Mousse

Make up a jelly with agar agar (as above). As you remove it from the heat, stir in a carton of cream or sour cream.

Allow to set.

RIBERRY

Syzygium luehmannii (syn. *Eugenia luehmannii*)

Other names: Cherry alder or satinash, clove lilly pilly, small-leaved eugenia, lilly pilly or watergum

CLIMATE	Temperate to tropical
HABITAT	Sandy soil near beaches and rainforests from Kempsey (NSW) to Cooktown (Qld)
FORM	Weeping evergreen rainforest tree, 5–7 m high, spreading 6–8 m
FOLIAGE	Small, glossy green, pointed leaves, 3–7 cm long, new growth bronze to vivid pink-red, purple or scarlet
FLOWERS	Small, fluffy white flowers in panicles, spring to summer
FRUITS	Pear-shaped, pink-red or purple-red fruits, 1–1.5 cm long, hanging in clusters, in summer

Riberry, with its spicy, clove-like flavour, is a favourite Australian native bushfood. Because of the demand, there are already about 5000 riberry bushes in commercial cultivation. The fruit is sought by bushfood restaurants because of its flavour and dull red colour and because it can be used whole, without removing the seeds, and most of the fruit is seedless.

The shiny leaves, an attractive bright pink-bronze in new growth turn glossy dark green and are tear-shaped, tapering to a point.

Growing
Riberry is probably the most popular widely grown rainforest tree. It is easy to propagate from fresh seed, but cuttings are hard to strike. Plants tolerate full sun and are fairly hardy in cultivation, but are frost-sensitive.

Like other lilly pillies, riberries will grow on a range of soils, but prefer good drainage and moisture. The trees reach 30 m in height in the wild, but rarely grow more than 10 m in cultivation. They are ornamental and often planted as street and park trees.

Eating
Riberries are incredibly versatile. The red fruits can be added to fruit salads, or mixed with peaches and plums in fruit crumbles, muffins or mixed with apples in strudels and scones. Riberries are related to cloves and taste a bit like them, which is why they are blended in sauces served with native meats like emu, kangaroo and quail.

The unusual taste of riberry sauce makes it good for pouring over puddings and ice cream.

Add riberries to vinegar or combine them with ginger in relishes and chutneys. Fruits freeze well, but will darken in colour. When cooked, they lose their colour, but regain it as they cool.

Riberries are good to glacé and use in fruit cakes. Mix with any other fruits in a compote, especially apples, pears or apricots.

Raymond Kersh of Sydney's famous restaurant 'Edna's Table', makes 'riberry jus' by boiling riberry fruit with wine, chicken stock, herbs and vinegar.

DESERT LIME

Eremocitrus glauca
Other names: Desert lemon, lime bush, native cumquat, wild lime

FAMILY	RUTACEAE
CLIMATE	Semi-arid
HABITAT	Dry forest, scrub and brigalow and along creek lines in arid parts of Qld, NSW and SA
FORM	Shrub or small tree, 2–6 m high, with thorny branches when young
FOLIAGE	Thick, green leaves, to 5 cm long. They will fall in dry spells
FLOWERS	White flowers have a citrus flower aroma, in spring
FRUITS	Small lime-green rounded fruits like small limes, 1–2 cm long, ripen in late spring and summer

Growing

Desert limes tolerate frost, drought and alkaline soil. They are best propagated by suckers, but will grow from seeds and make a good tub-plant.

Wild lime may bear fruit about four years after planting and sooner if grafted on ordinary citrus rootstock. They bear heavy crops.

The trees cross easily with cultivated citrus and are being investigated as a potential source of drought-resistant rootstock. Prune and remove suckers.

Eating

Desert limes have a soft rind and juicy pulp like cumquats. They can be eaten whole, and have a sour, strong citrus flavour with a slightly bitter aftertaste.

Put peeled fruit through a blender with sugar or honey and water to make a refreshing lemon drink. Fruit freezes well. Desert limes are used in much the same way as ordinary limes and are excellent for marinades, especially for fish and to make sauces and desserts.

FINGER LIME
Microcitrus australasica
Other names: Native lime

FAMILY	RUTACEAE
CLIMATE	Subtropical to warm temperate
HABITAT	Rainforests of Qld and northern NSW
FORM	Thorny deciduous shrub or small tree to 5 m high
FOLIAGE	Oval green leaves, 1–3 cm long
FLOWERS	Fragrant white flowers about 1 cm in diameter in autumn
FRUITS	Small, cylindrical, often curved citrus-like fruits, 5–6 cm long, may be green, yellow or purple when ripe

Growing
Finger limes will grow as far south as Sydney in frost-free areas. They need fertile, well-composted soil, plenty of moisture and slight shade. Propagate from fresh seed or cuttings. Bushes grow slowly to about 5 to 6 m in height and bear edible fruit in 4 to 5 years.

Finger lime is grafted on common citrus to breed improved rootstocks. A strain from Mullumbimby, NSW resists *citropthora* (citrus root fungus).

Eating
When you bite into the berries the sour pulp cells have a lemon flavour, with an oily aftertaste.

In the bush, settlers picked wild finger limes as a thirst quencher, or made them into fruit juice, which can be used like lemon juice. The limes make a tasty marmalade, with a distinctive flavour.

RELATED PLANTS
Pink-fleshed finger lime (*Microcitrus australasica* var. *sanguinea*)
This relative has pink flesh rather like that of blood oranges.

Round lime (*Microcitrus australis*)
Aboriginal name: Dooja (Qld)
The fruit is almost round, about 4 cm in diameter, with acid juice similar in flavour to the finger lime. An evergreen tree, found also in coastal rainforests of northern NSW and Qld. Leaves, about 4 to 5 cm long, are larger than those of the finger lime.

Mount White lime (*Microcitrus garrowayi*)
A tropical climate green finger lime from the Cape York (Qld) rainforest, it grows on a thorny-twigged tree which reaches 5 to 6 m in height.

Bears fragrant white flowers in spring. Fruit is like a small lemon, 6 cm long, with a sticky skin which smells of citrus when cut. Use for lime drinks or marmalade.

Russell River lime (*Microcitrus inodora*)
This citrus, found in north Qld rainforests, has oblong fruits about 6 cm long. F. M. Bailey, Colonial Botanist of Qld, found it growing while climbing Mt Bellenden Ker in 1889 and said it was 'well worthy ofcultivation for its fruit, which is juicy, and of equal flavour with the West Indian Lime'.

Best bushfruits for pies
Appleberry
Midyimberry
Muntries
Illawarra plum
Quandongs

MIDYIMBERRY
Austromyrtus dulcis (syn. *Myrtus tenuifolia*)
Aboriginal names: Midgen, midjin, midyim (Turrubul, Brisbane)
Other names: Midgenberry, midjinberry, silky myrtle

FAMILY   MYRTACEAE
CLIMATE   Temperate to tropical
HABITAT   Coastal heath and sandy islands from northern NSW to Fraser Island (Qld)

FORM	Low, spreading, mounded shrub, 50 cm–1 m tall and 80 cm wide
FOLIAGE	Paired, narrow, pointed leaves, 1–3 cm long, pink and silky when young, often bronze in cooler climates
FLOWERS	Masses of small, fluffy white flowers (like leptospermum flowers) form in the leaf axils in spring and summer
FRUIT	Round white, aromatic sweet berries, spotted with green-purple flecks, ripen twice (January and April)

Midyimberries are one of the most delicious Australian bushfruits. Plants belong to the vast myrtle family and are related to lilly pillies, muntries, eucalypts and lemon myrtle.

These sweet-tasting rounded, white, streaked fruits have loads of potential. Unfortunately, the berries are too soft to pack for transport to market. This gives a good reason to grow your own.

Midyimberries were a favourite food of the Undanbi and Noonucckal Aboriginal clans of the Brisbane River and the sandy islands of Moreton Bay. In 1836, Quaker missionary James Backhouse came across the 'sweet, aromatic berries' on the sandhills of Moreton Island and wrote: 'These are the most agreeable, native fruit, I have tasted in Australia; they are produced so abundantly, as to afford an important article of food, to the Aborigines.'

Historian Thomas Welsby was enchanted by the midyim bushes growing in the wallum (coastal vegetation) on Stradbroke Island. 'It springs up and grows like a wheat field ... one can go through acres of the shrub with its white, sweet-tasting berry until stopped by lagoon or salt water. It is the most sought-for berry or fruit on the island.' Aboriginal children, Welsby wrote, collected berries 'by the tin-full' and 'even the elders will join with gusto in its eating'.

Growing

Midyimberry bushes do best in a shady, sheltered place, in soil enriched with compost. However, plants will adapt to most soils, dry or moist, and full sun or part shade. They are frost-resistant.

The seed is viable for only a short time. Clean, fresh seed sown soon after eating the fruits should germinate in three or four weeks. Otherwise, propagate from cuttings or nursery stock. This is readily available.

These plants are slow-growing at first and need ample water. Fruit-yield is steady from the third year.

These compact and ornamental bushes, with striking pink-tipped young foliage, are used for ground cover or as screen plants for shaded sites. They are often seen in Brisbane gardens. We have a plant growing successfully in Sydney.

The fruit are soft and easily damaged when ripe, so handle them with care when picking.

Eating
Midyimberries are succulent and aromatic. Picked when ripe and eaten fresh they are soft and sweet, with just a slight resinous aftertaste. The skin is soft and the brown seeds are tiny, so the whole fruit can be eaten. Fruits are nice on a cheese platter.

Try midyimberries alone, or mixed with apples in pies, or made into jam.

RELATED PLANTS
Cape ironwood (*Austromyrtus floribunda*)
Bears abundant white flowers and small, edible black berries.

Narrow-leaved myrtle (*Austromyrtus tenuifolia*)
This plant has narrower leaves and smaller fruit than midyimberry. Habitat: Coastal forests of NSW.

Scrub ironwood (*Austromyrtus acmeniodes*)
A rainforest tree, with sharply-pointed leaves which can add flavour to tea.

Velvet myrtle (*Austromyrtus lasioclada*)
Velvet or scaly myrtle has woolly branches, rounded, glossy leaves and furry tips. Plants, which reach 1 to 4 m, bear pink and white summer flowers and black, olive-like fruit. Habitat: Richmond River (NSW) to Nambour (Qld).

M U N T R I E S

Kunzea pomifera

Evergreen

Aboriginal names: Munter, monterry, muntree, muntrey (Vic), ngurp, nurp (Bunganditj, Glenelg, Vic)

Other names: Crab apple, emu apple, muntari, muntaberry, munterberry, native cranberry

FAMILY	MYRTACEAE
CLIMATE	Temperate
HABITAT	Coastal and inland sand dunes and mallee from SA to Vic, including Kangaroo Island
FORM	Low, creeping shrub or ground cover, spreading 2–3 m
FOLIAGE	Small, glossy, dark green, stiff, oval leaves 0.5 cm long, with sharp curled tips
FLOWERS	Dense, fluffy, perfumed, creamy white, spiky blossoms, long-lasting, spring and early summer
FRUIT	Clusters of pea-sized berries, 1 cm in diameter, red-purple when ripe in late summer and autumn

Muntries bear fleshy, edible capsules which look, smell and taste like tiny apples. When ripe, the skin of the fruit is downy and tinged red, pink or purple, like a peach.

In western Vic, coastal Aborigines feasted on muntries in summer and took branches laden with fruit to their camps. In the Coorong area (now SA), fruit were dried and pounded into cakes and traded among the clans. Today, commercial plantations of muntries in SA are growing as many as 5000 plants.

Growing

Muntries are hardy and will tolerate frosts, salty conditions and strong sea winds and thrive in coastal gardens where there is little humidity. They fruit best in well-drained alkaline soils in full sunshine.

Excessive feeding with nitrogen fertiliser promotes growth but limits flower and fruit production.

Collect the fine seeds, which drop out of fruit drying on the tree. Sow from midwinter to spring in well-drained potting mix, with a light covering of sand. Seeds will germinate in 3 to 4 weeks.

To propagate from cuttings, take healthy, semi-ripe wood at any time of the year and strike in a sandy potting mix. Nodes or sections of wood in contact with moist earth will strike roots and make new plants. Plant seedlings 2 m apart, further away in dry places, and keep well-watered. It might take two or three years for plants to bear fruit regularly, but after that they will carry more than 1 kg per bush. Plants are susceptible to root rot.

Fertilise with a handful of blood and bone when the first fruits form.

Muntries are sold in nurseries as an ornamental ground cover. Creepers can be trellised for easier harvesting and respond well to tip-pruning in winter.

Eating

Muntries have a taste and texture like dried apples, with a hint of sultanas. Berries can be eaten fresh or in a fruit salad. They can be dried or frozen, but are better stewed or made into jam. Alternatively, they can be used in the same way as apples in tarts, pies, strudels and tea cakes.

Chutney made from Muntries, either alone or mixed with lemon myrtle chutney, is great with cold meats such as ham or cold sausages. Muntries sauce goes very well with hot dishes, particularly roast duck.

Bushfruit Chutney

Chutneys can be made with a combination of fruits, with no worries about pectin or acid levels.

A rough guide is to use about 4 kg of fruit to 1 kg of onions, 1 litre of vinegar and 1 kg of brown or raw sugar.

Spices, salt, pepper and sultanas or raisins can be added.

Use any combination of fruit, for example, various kinds of 'plums', lilly pillies, midyimberries, muntries, pigface fruit and quandong. Apples can be added if you don't have enough bushfruit.

Simmer the ingredients together until they form a thick pulp.

Caution: Do not use copper or brass pots or pans when making pickles or chutney, or for any recipe in which vinegar is used.

QUANDONG

Santalum acuminatum (syn. *Fusanus acuminatus*)
Aboriginal names: Bidjigal (Lake Hindmarsh, SA), beeticul (Lake Boga, Vic), gudi gudi, gutchu (Vic), guandang, qandang, quandong (Wiradjuri, NSW), mangata, mungata (Anangu, Uluru, NT), wajanu, wayanu (Pitjantjatjara, NT)
Other names: Desert quandong, desert peach, native peach, wild peach

FAMILY	SANTALACEAE
CLIMATE	Temperate to arid
HABITAT	Red desert sandhills and spinifex plains, near watercourses and salt lakes and in mulga country of inland Australia
FORM	Evergreen shrub or small tree, 4–5 m high
FOLIAGE	Narrow olive-green leaves 5–7 cm long, tapering to a point
FLOWERS	White to cream flowers in sprays, spring and summer
FRUITS	Plum-sized fruits turn from yellow-green to bright crimson when ripe
SEED	The hard stone is covered by a layer of white-yellow flesh

After weeks on a diet restricted to damper, anthropologist Charles Mountford (1890–1976) stumbled across a sandy valley in the desert near the Mann Ranges in Central Australia. It was dotted with wild peach (quandong) trees, their branches bending under the weight of scarlet fruit.

'Those peaches were a godsend!' Mountford recalled.

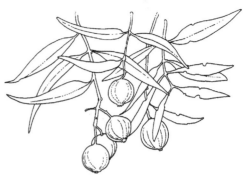

One month after he discovered the great rock monolith he named Ayer's Rock (now Uluru) in the Australian Central Desert, explorer William Gosse found quandong bushes laden with ripe fruit on the banks of a dry creek. Gosse, leader of a camel mounted expedition, boiled up the fruit to make jam and ward off scurvy. 'It is the prettiest fruit I have seen growing,' Gosse wrote in his journal for August 1873.

The fruits of the quandong have sustained countless generations of Aborigines. In the Western Desert, they were the staple diet of the Pitjantjatjara and Pintubi. Quandong is a Wiradjuri Aboriginal word from south-western NSW.

Quandongs, which are endangered by heavy grazing by camels and livestock, have been successfully domesticated after years of research and trials by the CSIRO.

There are already more than 40 000 trees, ranging from one to five years old, in commercial plantations. Of these, 25 000 trees have been planted in SA, 5000 at Shoalmarra Outback Australian Fruit Farm (Ben and Natalie McNamara) at Tumby Bay on the Eyre Peninsula, 2000 in Victoria's north-west mallee sands, and others around Broken Hill (NSW). More grow in the CSIRO's experimental orchards at Quorn (SA), at Mildura (Vic) and in home gardens around Alice Springs (NT).

The major problem scientists had to face was that the young quandong is a partial root parasite and depends on a host plant for its nutrients. The quandong is related to sandalwood, but the trees droop more.

Growing

Quandongs grow best in sandy red desert soil and will tolerate saline soil and salty bore water. They are drought-tolerant once established and do not require cold to be able to germinate. But germination is difficult.

If you crack one year old stones open in a vice and clean the kernels in diluted household bleach and plant them immediately they should come up quickly. Otherwise, put the seeds in a plastic bag filled with moist sawdust, ashes and peat and keep in a warm place. When the white sprout emerges, plant in pots or directly where bushes are to grow. Uncracked seeds can take one year to germinate.

Plant out quandongs in spring or autumn when 15 to 30 cm tall. They must be close to a host plant, which should be a perennial, for example, native grasses, spinifex, kikuyu, lucerne and other shrubs or trees, especially citrus. Running postman (*Kennedia prostrata*) has also been used as a host.

The trees grow slowly, but will bear within four years and should produce prolifically after that.

A range of seedling plants to suit all Australian climates is now available.

Eating

Many books say that quandong fruits are leathery, acid and sour. We ate fruits straight from the trees in the wild in Central Australia and found them soft, sweet, juicy and delicious, with a taste somewhere between apricot and peach.

The vitamin C content per gram is twice that of an orange. Most bushfruits contain very little water, so the flesh is very concentrated.

Fresh quandongs can be mixed with other fruits such as figs and bananas or fresh ginger. Cooked, apple and quandong makes a fantastic pie filling or jam mix.

Quandong flesh, when removed from the large central stone, can be made into fruit leathers or frozen for later use.

To dry quandongs, cut fruit in half and remove the pitted stones with a sharp knife. Place cut fruit on trays and leave them in the sun (or near the kitchen stove) for 5 to 7 days. Dried fruit, raw or roasted, contains good protein. To rehydrate dried fruit, soak in water, two or three hours before cooking and boil up in the same water. Dried quandongs are readily available.

Seed necklaces

Large, deeply-pitted blue quandong or quandong stones make pretty necklaces.

Clean fresh seeds by soaking them in water for two or three weeks until they are soft. Then, drill a hole through the stones with hot wire and thread them on twine.

Stones are also used in such games as Chinese checkers and marbles and as game counters.

The kernels of the nuts of this small tree are not only palatable and nutritious, but they are so full of oil that if speared on a stick or reed they will burn entirely away with a clear light, much in the same way as candle-nuts do.

Joseph Maiden, *The Useful Native Plants of Australia*, Sydney, 1889

Nuts
Desert Aborigines usually roast the hard, pitted quandong kernels and know how long to wait until the toxic element in them is dissipated by decay but we don't so we don't recommend eating them. Pitjantjatjara lightly roast whole kernels in hot ashes and eat them when they turn black.

The edible nuts contain 25 per cent protein and 70 per cent oil. Nuts are used to make necklaces, bracelets and Chinese checker pieces.

Quandong Sauce

Cook dried quandong fruits for a few minutes in a small amount of water, with a dash of lemon or orange juice and sugar or honey to taste.

Leave in the refrigerator overnight. Reheat if needed. This sauce can be poured over ice cream or pancakes, or used as a sauce with meat and chicken.

RELATED PLANTS
Plum bush (*Santalum lanceolatum*)
Aboriginal names: Arnguli (Anangu, Uluru, NT),
tharrah, gibberah (Cloncurry River, Qld)
Other names: Bush plum, northern sandalwood

The graceful trees grow 2 to 3 m high. Small oval fruits are ripe when they become black-purple and can be eaten raw, dried, after soaking in water. The stones are eaten when roasted. Blue-grey wood is perfumed.
Habitat: Foot of hills in the dry inland, including Vic.

ROSE MYRTLE
Archirhodomyrtus beckleri (syn. *Rhodomyrtus beckleri*)
Aboriginal names: Gingul (Richmond River, NSW), kaarin (unknown)
Also called: Pink myrtle

FAMILY	MYRTACEAE
CLIMATE	Temperate to tropical
HABITAT	Rainforests from Newcastle (NSW) to Cairns (north Qld)
FORM	Shrub, 1–1.5 m tall and wide
FOLIAGE	Aromatic, glossy, small, elliptical leaves with slightly waved edges, 4–11 cm long
FLOWERS	Shell pink, perfumed flowers, borne in leaf axils, in spring and early summer
FRUITS	Orange-red berry fruits, up to 1 cm long, summer and autumn

Rose myrtle is an elegant, rounded shrub which grows in high rainforests and around rainforest edges in less fertile soils. Its glossy, aromatic leaves contain translucent oil glands, which can be seen by holding up a leaf to the light.

This plant was named after Dr Herman Beckler, botanist and medical officer to the ill-fated Burke and Wills expedition of 1860. He left the party after crossing the Darling River.

Growing

Rose myrtle will grow successfully in full or semi-shade, in a moist but well-drained place. Once established, shrubs will tolerate cool conditions and even light frosts. Cuttings strike quickly and seed is reliable, though slow to germinate.

Excess moisture and fertilising will bring a flush of growth to the foliage, but results in less flowers and fruit.

Rose myrtle makes an elegant container plant.

Eating

Sue Forster and Bill Molyneux of Austraflora, who are developing the plant commercially, say the fruit is delicious, and makes a lovely sticky jam. The leaves may be dried and used in soups and stews for a tangy flavouring.

CHAPTER 3

Bush Vegetables

Yummy yams There are only a few bushfoods which most people would consider as vegetables. However, we do have indigenous tomatoes, potatoes, yams and some leafy greens. Warrigal greens are perhaps the easiest leafy vegetable to grow in the world. They mix well with our common, 'foreign' vegetables, both in the garden and on the plate.

BUSH TOMATO

Solanum centrale

Aboriginal names: Aakajirri, akatjera, akatjira, akudjura (Pitjantjatjara, Central Australia), akatjirra, akatyerr (Alyawarra, Utopia, NT), akaty-erre (Arrernte, NT), kati kati, kampurarpa, kumbararapa (Anangu, Uluru, NT), yakajirri (Warlpiri, NT)

Other names: Bush raisin, desert raisin

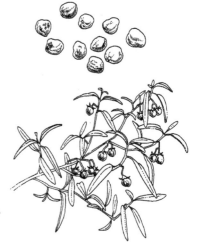

FAMILY	SOLANACEAE
CLIMATE	Arid and semi-arid to warm temperate
HABITAT	Red sandhills and spinifex sand plains of Central Australia
FORM	Low, straggly shrub, 20–45 cm high with soft, furry or prickly stems
FOLIAGE	Oval, light green when young, changing to olive-green, 3–4 cm long
FLOWERS	Star-shaped pale or deep purple flowers, which bloom after rain
FRUITS	Sticky, globular fruits, about 1 cm in diameter, hang in clusters under the leaves, turning from green to white, then yellow as they ripen in spring and summer. When dried they resemble dark brown raisins

There are many species of wild Australian bush tomatoes. They belong to the *Solanum* family, like ordinary tomatoes, but not all are edible, and some, which contain the alkaloid *solanine*, are poisonous. They are low, bushy shrubs, with purple flowers and small fruits which dry and shrivel on the bush and are consequently called desert sultanas or raisins.

Fruits of the common bush tomato (*Solanum centrale*) can be eaten with their seeds, but the bitter black seeds of the green bush tomato (*Solanum chippendali*) must be removed before eating or drying.

Bush tomatoes are often found growing in places which have been burnt by Aborigines in the previous season. Heavy crops occur in the second year after a fire and also after rains. In the desert, Aborigines used wild tomato fruits as a source of water.

In 1997 there were about 12 000 bush tomato shrubs planted commercially in Australia, mostly in SA.

Growing

Bush tomatoes are propagated by seeds from mature or dried fruit. They look just like ordinary tomato seeds but are often difficult to germinate. Because plants regenerate after fire, we've tried burning and smoking seeds on the barbecue, but don't have any definite results as yet.

They are grown in the same way as ordinary tomatoes.

The fruits are bigger when raised in temperate climates and on fertile soil.

In the wild, bushes are so low that tomatoes hanging from the branches often lie on the sand, so in home gardens, put down a layer of mulch to protect them.

Desert Aborigines scatter the seeds on the burnt areas of land near their campfires.

Eating

Bush tomatoes have a mildly hot, spicy taste and can be eaten raw, although, according to Peter Latz (1995), you might get a headache if you eat too many at one time.

Left to dry on the bush, or collected after they fall to the ground, they become wrinkled and red-brown and look like large raisins. They have a firm, fleshy texture and soft, edible seeds, like those of sun-dried tomatoes and a strong, spicy, slightly bitter aroma and flavour that is unique.

Dried bush tomatoes are being used in all kinds of modern dishes. We suggest that you store some finely chopped in the pantry, ready to use. They complement any dish in which tomatoes are normally used, such as pasta and casseroles, and can be chopped into salad dressings. They can also be added to soups, quiches, pizza and frittata or made into chutney, sauce or salsa and chilli jam.

A coarse, crumbly powder is made by grinding up the dried fruit using a food processor or mortar and pestle. The powder is now readily available and known as akudjura, one of the Central Australian Aboriginal names for the bush tomato. Use this powder as a spice, sprinkled, like paprika or pepper, over pasta, pizza or fish, or mix a pinch into soft cheese, stews and goulash.

Bush Tomato Balls

In Central Australia, passers-by eat wild bush tomato fruits from the bushes while the fruits are unripe. They are also collected and brought into camp by women and children who gather *mai* (vegetables, fruits and seeds).

Among the Anangu at Uluru (Ayers Rock) and the Walpiri (further south), fruits which dry on the bush are cleaned, crushed to a crumbly powder by pounding with stones, then mixed with water and pressed into a ball of round pulp, which is called a *kaputu*.

The brown balls (which include the seeds) are sometimes covered with a thin layer of red ochre. Traditionally, these bright balls were wrapped in paperbark packets then dried in the sun, and stored in the fork of a tree or on top of a bark shelter. They were often traded in ceremonial exchanges, and this helped to spread the seeds.

When soaked in water, the dried balls are reconstituted into a red-brown paste which has a jam-like consistency.

If you grow your own bush tomatoes, you can preserve them in this way. Do not dry or eat the seeds of green bush tomatoes.

GREEN BUSH TOMATO

Solanum chippendalei
Aboriginal names: Nganjanvarli, wanakiji (Warlpiri, NT), wiriny-wirinipa (Pitjantjatjara, NT)
Other names: Bush sultana, bush tomato

FAMILY	SOLANACEAE
CLIMATE	Arid to warm temperate
HABITAT	Mulga and spinifex bushland of arid Central Australia
FORM	Low, shrubby bush
FOLIAGE	Prickly stems
FLOWERS	Small, purple, potato-like flowers
FRUITS	Fruits turn from white to yellow when ripe and sweet

The Walpiri at Yuendumu (NT) are familiar with several different varieties of green bush tomatoes.

> **Caution**
> Before eating green bush tomatoes, you must remove the black seeds, which are bitter and possibly toxic.

Eating

Green bush tomatoes should be picked when they are yellow and sweet.

The dry, wrinkled fruits can be gathered from the ground under the bushes. They have a high vitamin C content. The skins (without seeds) can be dried in the sun and stored on strings, or the skins and halves (without seeds) threaded on thick stick skewers to dry in the sun or by the campfire.

Dried green bush tomatoes are reconstituted by soaking them in water. They can be lightly cooked in the coals of a fire.

PIGFACE

Carpobrutus rossi
Aboriginal names: Canajong (Tas), karkalla (Port Lincoln, SA), cutwort, katwort, nakalu (Gippsland, Vic)
Other names: Coastal pigface, Ross's noonflower

FAMILY	AIZOACEAE
CLIMATE	Temperate
HABITAT	Beaches, dunes, cliffs and inland areas of SE and SW Australia
FORM	Prostrate, creeping ground cover with trailing branches to 2 m long
FOLIAGE	Succulent, three-sided, blue-green leaves, sometimes red
FLOWERS	Large purple flowers in spring and throughout the year
FRUITS	Small, fleshy, pulpy fruit, shaped like a pig's head, ripe when red-purple, late summer

Pigface plants belong to the same botanical family as Warrigal greens.

'When ripe, the fruit is rich, juicy, and sweet, and about the size of a gooseberry,' wrote explorer Edward John Eyre. Pigface was 'a favourite and important article of food among the native population near Fowler's Bay [SA],' Eyre noted on his expedition to the Great Australian Bight in 1840.

Aborigines around Port Lincoln (SA) pressed the fleshy fruits of pigface between their fingers to squeeze the juice into their mouths. 'The men,' wrote Joseph Maiden (1889), 'generally gather only as much as they want for the moment, but the women collect large quantities for eating after supper.'

Growing

Pigface tolerates dry conditions and frosts and resists drought. It commonly grows on the coast and is used to stabilise sand dunes.

Propagate plants from cuttings or divided layers, set out about 1 m apart in full sun in sandy or well-drained soil. The plants spread thickly over rocks and hang over walls.

Pick fruit fresh, before the leaves have withered, or after the fruit has dried.

Eating

Aborigines in Victoria ate the salty leaves of pigface as a kind of relish with meat and other foods. The leaves can be cooked in a stir-fry.

Break off ripe fruit and suck out the small seeds and pulp. The taste has been compared to salty figs or apples. European settlers made pigface fruit into jam, pickles or chutney. See **Pickled bushfruit**, p.57.

RELATED PLANTS

Similar species of pigface grow in various parts of Australia and also in southern Africa and South America.

Noonflower (*Carpobrutus aequilaterus*)
Prostrate, fleshy pigface, 10 to 15 cm high, spreading to 3 m, found along the rocky seacoast of Australia and in sandy inland areas. Large, creamy flowers turn purple from spring to autumn. Reddish edible fruits.

Coastal noonflower (*Carpobrutus glaucescens*)
Grows on coastal sand dunes in NSW and Qld. Similar to the noonflower.

Inland pigface (*Carpobrutus modestus*)

A drought-resistant pigface of the dry inland, which will grow elsewhere in well-drained soil. Bears blue-green or reddish leaves and sweet, jelly-like fruits.

Habitat: Vic, SA, WA.

Bain or coastal pigface (*Carpobrutus virescens*)

Aboriginal name: Bain (Nyungar, WA)

A prostrate, shrubby pigface of coastal SW Australia and offshore islands, with trailing 2 m long red-grey branches and green or red fleshy leaves. In spring they bear bright pink-mauve flowers with a white centre.

PIGWEED

Portulaca oleracea

Aboriginal names Plants: Kurumba (Bourke, NSW), mangurlu (Gurinji, NT), munyeroo (Cooper's Creek), thukouro (Cloncurry River, Qld), wakati (Pitjantjatjara, NT). Seeds: Kunaurra (Cooper's Creek), ntange ulyawe (Arrernte, NT), wilarra (Gurinji, NT)

Other names: Inland pigweed, pussly (USA), wild purslane

FAMILY	PORTULACEAE
CLIMATE	Arid and temperate to tropical
HABITAT	Widespread on sand ridges and plains, river-banks, mulga country and in disturbed soil
FORM	Succulent annual or perennial plant, with red-brown stems 40 cm long, which lie flat on the ground
FOLIAGE	Wedge-shaped, fleshy leaves, with rounded tips, 1–2.5 cm long
FLOWERS	Small yellow flowers, solitary or in clusters in leaf forks, summer
FRUITS	Small capsules with pointy 'caps', filled with tiny seeds (smaller than poppy seeds), after rain
SEEDS	The pitted and shiny kidney-shaped jet black seeds contain oil

Pigweed, which is not related to pigface (*Carpobrutus* species), got its unlovely name because foraging pigs are fond of it. Seeds, leaves and stalks can all be eaten.

These wild greens sustained the ill-fated nineteenth-century explorers, Robert O'Hara Burke and William John Wills and also Ludwig Leichhardt, who wrote in 1884 that he had enjoyed 'some fine messes' of it. The greens are nutritious and were believed in the past to prevent scurvy, which is caused by a deficiency of vitamin C. Recent analysis shows that they contain very little of the vitamin.

The seeds, a staple food of desert Aborigines, contain 18 to 20 per cent protein, more than wholemeal bread (11.5 per cent) and double that of rice (6.9 per cent). 'The Aborigines', wrote Joseph Maiden (1889), 'get in splendid condition on it.'

Growing

Pigweed is very hardy and will grow in all climates and in most kinds of soil, in a sunny, well-drained spot. Plants grow prolifically after brief summer rains in arid places and following the Wet season in the tropical Top End.

Sow the seeds in spring, when there is no danger of frost.

Growing plants will survive dry spells and salt spray and need little care once they are established. Plants reseed each year and spread wildly. In the bushfood garden, pigweed can be used as a ground cover, low hedge, edging, or between paving stones.

Eating

Greens   The succulent, rather slimy, slightly bitter and spicy leaves and stems are eaten as a green vegetable. The leaf tips are tastier when picked before flowers develop, after which the stems become tough. Add raw young shoots to salads or steam or boil the greens like spinach. Try pigweed greens in stir-fries or add to soups as a thickener.

Aborigines mash the raw shoots and leaves into balls of paste which they eat raw, or dried and reconstituted by adding water. They also roast the fleshy stalks in ashes to soften the tough taproot for eating.

Seeds   Collect seeds when the stems change colour from green to pink.

Aborigines pull up mature plants from a wide area, pile them in heaps, and leave them to dry on sheets of bark. The bushes are later turned over to dry further. Seeds are released as the capsules dry. They are gathered and cleaned by yandying (tossing up and down) in a coolamon or other container to remove the small capsule caps. Another method is to place plants over a container and agitate them gently to release the seeds.

The clean seeds are mashed into a coarse paste between two flat stones and shaped into small cakes which can be eaten raw, but are usually baked in hot sand, fire ashes or coals. Oil from the linseed-like seeds leaves a shiny coating on the grinding stones. Add pigweed seeds to the dough mix for breads and rolls or sprinkle on food instead of poppy seeds.

RELATED PLANTS
Inland pigweed (*Portulaca australis*)
A Top End plant which has narrower leaves and is used in the same way as common pigweed.

Purslane or golden purslane (*Portulaca oleracea* var. *sativa*)
The garden pigweed has been grown for centuries in Europe, where it is a common weed. Plants are more erect and larger than the wild Australian plant, and have rounded, 4 cm wide, thick, succulent green leaves on golden stems. The leaves have a mild flavour and very high vitamin C content and are used in salads or as a pot herb. Pick tender young shoots when they are 3 to 5 cm long.

WARRIGAL GREENS
Tetragonia tetragoniodes (syn. *Tetragonia expansa*; *T. cornuta*)
Other names: Botany Bay greens, New Zealand spinach, Sydney greens, warrigal cabbage; kokihi (Maori, New Zealand), tetragon (France), tsuruna (Japan)

FAMILY	AIZOACEAE
CLIMATE	Temperate to tropical
HABITAT	Sandy and stony beaches, sand dunes and salt marshes along the coasts of Australia, New Zealand, Lord Howe and other Pacific Islands; also inland plains
FORM	Low, spreading perennial vine with thick, succulent stems
FOLIAGE	Arrowhead-shaped, soft, flat, shiny, dark green leaves to 8 cm
FLOWERS	Tiny, yellow, star-shaped flowers in leaf axils, spring and summer

A mass of thick, soft, dark-green leaves served as a salad or a side dish of greens has begun to appear in Australian restaurants and cafes whose chefs include native 'bush tucker' ingredients in thei menus.'New Zealand spinach' was the first Australian native food plant to be introduced into Europe, late in the eighteenth century. In October 1769 this 'wild spinach' was found growing at Queen Charlotte Sound on the New Zealand coast by a shore party from HMS *Endeavour*. Seeds were taken home to Kew Gardens by Joseph Banks in 1772.

Warrigal greens, the new marketing name for this Australian herb, seems to have been coined from two older ones, Warrigal Cabbage and Botany Bay Greens. Warrigal was the Eora (Sydney area) Aboriginal name for the native dog or dingo.

These nutritious greens were added to the scant rations of the first British settlers at Sydney Cove in 1788. 'There is a Plant very like the Spinage in England which afford us a very good repast with a piece of — I was going to say Pork, but will call it Bacon,' wrote Lieutenant Newton Fowell of HMS *Sirius*.

On his way by boat to Parramatta in March 1793, the Spanish botanist Don Luis Née jumped ashore at Kissing Point (now Ryde) on the Parramatta River. 'I had hardly touched ground when I found two tetragonias and various other oraches, all edible, as I pointed out to the colonists,' Née wrote in his journal.

'Botany Bay greens are procured in abundance,' wrote David Dickinson Mann in *The Present Picture of New South Wales* (London, 1811), 'and are esteemed a very good dish by the Europeans, but despised by the natives.' Seeds of 'New Zealand Spinach' were sent to the new settlement at King George's Sound, Albany, in WA in November 1826. In London, seedsmen Flanagan & Nutting offered 'New Zealand, or Tetragona Expansa' in their 1835 catalogue.

Warrigal greens are widely grown in home vegetable gardens in Australia and commercial quantities have been planted to supply restaurants and bushfood suppliers. It is grown as a summer spinach in

Britain and the United States and is popular in France where it is called *tetragon*.

Tiny yellow star-flowers in the bracts between the leaves ripen into hard seed containers in warm weather.

Growing

Warrigal greens are easy to grow from seed and make a good substitute for the 'true' or English spinach to which they are not related. They adapt to hot, dry and sandy soils and resist salt spray. Once established, plants resist drought and provide year-round 'cut and come again' crops in all but the coldest climates.

Before planting, in spring and summer, pour hot water over the seeds and leave them to soak overnight. Next day, sow them about 60 cm apart in a shady spot, and just cover them with soil or compost. In cool places, sow seed in pots under glass and transplant seedlings to the garden when there is no danger of frost.

The plants mature in about 10 weeks, but you can pinch off the young shoots and leaves for eating—and keep on picking them through summer and autumn. If you allow one or two plants to set seed, new plants will spring up each year.

Plants need little water except in very dry weather.

Warrigal greens, like lettuce, can be grown without soil using the hydroponic method.

Eating

Lightly blanch warrigal leaves to remove mildly toxic oxalates. Blanch the leaves in boiling water for about one minute, then plunge them into cold water immediately. This will keep their green colour. Drain. Discard the water.

Wilted warrigal greens make an attractive, colourful bed for a kumara patty or a piece of barbecued fish. Use young leaves in salads. The slightly tart flavour will be lifted by a touch of lemon juice or a French salad dressing.

Older, bigger leaves are too tough and clammy to eat raw, but are delicious in soup or cooked like baby spinach. Cook and then blend with onions and potatoes and serve hot or cold. Thin with milk, if necessary.

Try fresh warrigal greens with bush tomato chutney or in a *pesto* sauce with macadamia or bunya nuts.

Bushfood Salad
Mix together blanched warrigal greens, tomato wedges and any bush-fruits you might have. Dress with macadamia oil and vinegar.

Warrigal Pie
Pick warrigal greens, other garden greens such as Good King Henry, mizuna, mibuna and silver beet; edible 'weeds' like dandelion, dock and fat hen; and any herbs on hand. Wash, shred and steam greens to use as a pie filling.

Oz Pasta
Mix cooked pasta with wilted warrigal greens and top with a sauce made from onion, tomato, bush tomato and bushfruits like muntries.

RELATED PLANTS

Bower spinach (*Tetragonia implexicoma*)
Bower spinach or ice plant is not as tasty as warrigal greens, but was eaten by early settlers to guard against scurvy.

Creepers, with small yellow flowers and red-black berries, form dense mats on sandy beaches in the cool temperate southern states.

Use the succulent leaves in the same way as warrigal greens. The berries are said to be sweet when ripe. Propagate from cuttings and grow in well-drained soil.

Roots and tubers
Bush yams and potatoes were an important food resource for Aborigines throughout Australia, especially in the Central Desert and the tropical north.

Warrine yam was a favourite root crop of the Nyungar around Perth (WA). The Dharug, who lived in the inland areas around Sydney, tended yam beds on both sides of the Hawkesbury River.

In SA and Vic, tubers of lily, orchid and yam daisies were treated as staple foods by Aboriginal people. They are low in fat and high in carbohydrate and dietary fibre. The roots also contain sodium, potassium, calcium and magnesium.

Digging sticks

Aboriginal women made their own implements for gathering food. Their prized digging sticks, always carried with them, could also be used as a weapon and were often buried beside them.

Digging for yams.

The sticks were made from long, straight mulga branches, 30 cm to 2 m long. They were shaped and smoothed with cutting stones and sharpened by fire to a chisel point at one end. Archaeologists have unearthed two wooden digging sticks about 9000 years old, preserved in the Wyrie swamps (SA).

'Plants supplied so much of the food eaten in many parts of Australia that the digging stick rather than the spear was the vital implement,' wrote historian Geoffrey Blainey in *Triumph of the Nomads* (Melbourne, 1976).

The use of their digging sticks aerated the soil, thinned out root clumps and spread pieces of root over a wide area. Mardu women of the Great Western Desert (WA) always left the old 'mother tuber' in the ground, others replaced part of a yam tuber to ensure future crops.

In northern Australia today, metal rods like crowbars (*kurupa*: Pitjantjatjara), about 70 cm long and with one end hammered flat, have replaced wooden digging sticks.

Digging sticks, new and old.

BUSH YAMS
FAMILIES   DIOSCOREACEAE and CONVOLVULACEAE

The aerial stems of Australian native yams are thin and wiry and climb by twining. Their leaves are heart-shaped and net-veined. The edible tubers are found deep in the soil, up to 50 cm or more under the ground. Some yams are long and narrow, while others are elongated, plump, round or shaped like parsnips.

Caution: many species of bush yams are toxic. Leach them before use by slicing and soaking for a long time in running water.

Growing

It's good to go foraging with a digging stick in your own backyard.

The majority of yams grow in arid or tropical areas. Tubers take about nine months to mature. They can be left in the ground for about two months after they mature and dug out as needed. Small yams can be put back in the ground to grow bigger.

Tubers without broken skin will keep well, so they can be eaten for most of the year. Heap them up, heads upwards, on the floor or on shelves in a dry, sheltered place.

Propagate by dividing tubers (called setts) or by planting whole tubers. These are difficult to obtain, so if you get some, share them around. In cultivation, allow 75 cm to 1 m between plants. Vines may be trained on bamboo or wooden stakes or trellises or over fences and pergolas (best for aerial potatoes). Mulch around the base of vines to keep weeds down.

Make sure you keep a few of the healthiest yams for seed. If stored yams start to put out shoots, they are ready to plant.

Eating

Bush yams and potatoes are chewy, fibrous and starchy ('floury'), with a rather tart taste, cheeky yams are hot and peppery.

Cooked yams taste like kumara or sweet potatoes and can be used in the same way.

Try them baked in paperbark sheets with fish or yabbies.

LONG YAM

Dioscorea transversa (syn. *D. sativa* var. *elongata*)
Aboriginal names: Kowar (central Qld), marndakirriyrra (Groote Eylandt, Qld), midiny (Eora, Sydney), ganguri (Arnhemland, NT), tarm (Turrubul, Brisbane, Qld), towwack (north Qld)
Other names: Parsnip yam

CLIMATE	Temperate to tropical
HABITAT	Common yam of coastal rainforest from Sydney to Cape York and across northern Australia
FORM	Tall, twining creeper with fine, smooth stems
FOLIAGE	Heart-shaped, shiny, smooth, lobed and veined leaves, smaller than those of *D. bulbifera*

FLOWERS	February to March
FRUITS	Pale green three-angled winged seedpods hang in clusters behind the leaves
TUBERS	Small, slender, white tubers, to 60 cm long, grow deep under the earth

In the wild, these long tubers are found at the edges of the rainforest. They were relished by the Aborigines who lived on the Bloomfield River in north Qld. They sliced and soaked them in water for several hours before baking them.

Eating
Long yams have a similiar taste to a potato, but are waxier and very tasty when roasted. Like other native yams, they are delicious cooked with meat and other vegetables in a Maori style *hangi*, or pit oven.

CHEEKY YAM

Dioscorea bulbifera (syn. *D. sativa* var. *rotunda*)
Aboriginal names: Gunu (Kimberleys, WA), jitama (East Arnhemland, NT), karoo (Mitchell River, Qld), wukay (Bloomfield River, Qld)
Other names: Hairy yam, round yam

CLIMATE	Tropical
HABITAT	Rainforest, rocky outcrops sandy soils of the Top End, from Arnhemland to Cape York; also Melanesia, Asia and Africa
FORM	Running vines with stems which twist to the right and cover trees
FOLIAGE	Large, heart-shaped, veined, shiny leaves
FLOWERS	Flowers like orchids hang down from vines
TUBERS	Round, fat, hairy, black tubers with yellow flesh, 5–12 cm in diameter, are edible, but toxic unless soaked well before being eaten

Eating

'Cheeky' is Aboriginal-English slang which refers both to the spicy hot or peppery taste of the hairy round yam and to the fact that they are poisonous.

These yams must be prepared before eating by scraping off the skin and hairs. You can do it over an open flame. The tubers are then cut into slices about 1 cm thick and either boiled or roasted in a bush oven or under fire ashes for several hours or overnight. Otherwise, they are first cooked and then leached of toxins by soaking them in running water for 6–24 hours.

Cheeky yams contain high amounts of vitamin C, some fat and carbohydrate. They taste like potatoes with a spicy, 'floury' edge and make excellent yam cakes.

The bulbils which form on the vines are sometimes eaten when they turn white.

RELATED PLANTS

Aerial yam (*Dioscorea bulbifera*)
Other names: Aerial potato
Some types of yam vines, including variants of D. *bulbifera*, have bulbils or aerial tubers which grow off the ground in the axils of their very large leaves. One tuber may yield 10 hanging 'potatoes' with purple flesh. Vine stems twist to the right. They are found in subtropical southern Qld.

They must be washed and cooked and many wild forms are toxic.
Maturity: 8 to 11 months.

BUSH POTATO

Ipomoea costata
Aboriginal name: Anatye (Arrernte, NT), pikuta (Gurinji, NT), yala, yarla (Central Desert)
Other names: Bush yam, cow vine, desert yam, rock morning glory

FAMILY	CONVOLVULACEAE
CLIMATE	Arid to tropical
HABITAT	Spinifex sand plains and hills and mulga of NW Central Australia
FORM	Vine or shrub to 1 m, with long, trailing branches

FOLIAGE	Smooth, leathery, broad green, veined leaves, 4–9 cm long
FLOWERS	Large, showy flowers, pink with a red throat, after rain in summer
TUBERS	Large, rounded root tubers, 12–50 cm long and 5–8 cm wide, with whitish skin when young and fibrous brown skin when old

The bush potato is not really a yam, but the root of a plant belonging to the Morning Glory or sweet potato botanical family. These roots or tubers are traditional tucker for Aborigines in Central Australia, where *yarla* is the name for the yam ancestors, and they often feature in Dreaming stories and paintings.

The tubers are hard to find as they grow well away from the main stem and deep below the surface. They can be traced by the long runners or 'strings' leading down to the tuber, or through tell-tale cracks in the sand around the plant.

The best tubers are found up to 3 m away from the main stem and up to 1 m below the surface. Those right under the stem are usually old and woody. Each plant may produce 20 or more 'yams'. Large ones can be as big as a man's head but the small ones are sweeter.

Eating
Bush potatoes are good tucker, say the Gurinji, who eat the tubers raw or roasted. When young and juicy, bush potatoes are sweet, with a crisp texture, just like sweet potatoes and eaten in the same way. Other desert clans like to cook the tubers in the fire ashes and peel them before eating, though the skin is tasty. Bush potatoes are 50 per cent water and are much valued in the desert.

WARRAIN
Dioscorea hastifolia
Aboriginal names: Warran, warrane, warrany, warrien, warrine, wirang (Nyungar, WA)

Other names: Native potato, native yam, warran yam

CLIMATE	Temperate
HABITAT	Fertile soils of SW Australia, from Sharks Bay south to Perth
FORM	Scrambling or twining shrub to 2 m
FOLIAGE	Long, thin leaves, 2 cm wide, may reach 8 cm in length
FLOWERS	Male and female flowers, winter
FRUITS	Only female flowers produce winged fruits, about 2 cm long
TUBERS	Yams are cylindrical and about 2–3 cm in diameter. They can be collected after the first rains (April to May) and from October to November

The thin tendrils of warrain twine over rocks and stony ground through-out SW Australia, where it was a staple food. Studies show that warrain tubers are almost 5 per cent protein. It is believed that they have been dug and cultivated by the Nyungar people for 5000 years.

These yams grew prolifically in the area around Perth. Explorer George Grey (1841) found 'tracts of land of several square miles in extent, so thickly studded with holes, where the natives had been digging up yams, that it was difficult to walk across it'. Settlers found it was even more dangerous to ride horses through the Nyungar yam fields.

Growing
Warrain plants bear male and female flowers, but only the female ones are followed by green winged seed pods. Tubers are like long thin potatoes.

Eating
'It has a sweet and delicate flavour when roasted in the hot ashes and is much sought after,' wrote surveyor Phillip Snell Chauncy (1876).

YAM DAISY
Microseris lanceolata (syn. *Microseris forsteri*)
Aboriginal names: Mirr-n'yong, murnong, murr-nong (Geelong,Vic) muurang, myrnong (Vic), yerat (Lake Condah, Vic)
Other names: Murnong, native dandelion

FAMILY	ASTERACEAE
CLIMATE	Temperate
HABITAT	Grassy, open plains and forests of SE Australia, including Tas
FORM	Small, clumpy perennial plant, reaching 10–30 cm in height; dormant from midsummer to spring
FOLIAGE	Long, narrow, finely-toothed bright green leaves
FLOWERS	In spring the drooping buds are followed by deep yellow, daisy-like flowers with strap-shaped florets
SEEDS	The flowers turn into a dandelion-like blow ball in summer
TUBERS	White-fleshed, sweet, tuberous roots, shaped like parsnips, 1–2.5 cm long, mature spring to early summer

The fleshy tuber of the yam daisy has perhaps the most potential of any Australian bushfood. It is at the same stage of development as carrots were about 400 years ago, when they were short, stumpy, hairy purple roots which stained cooking pots.

The yam daisy is a vanishing plant that we can help to preserve in our bushfood gardens. Yam daisy tubers will be improved by crossing different strains to increase the size and number of the tubers. In time, we think, they will take their place on the supermarket shelves next to more familiar root vegetables.

It has pretty yellow flowers, more like dandelions than daisies. A small, purple-skinned and white-fleshed milky tuber, round like a radish or tapered like a small baby carrot or parsnip forms a few cm below the ground.

The taste of the tuber has been likened to sweet potatoes, parsnips and scorzonera, the 'vegetable oyster', which is a valuable but neglected European vegetable. When slowly roasted, the tubers produce a dark, sweet, thick syrup which tastes like coconut.

For countless generations, yam daisies, ground orchids and lilies were the main staple foods of the Aboriginal clans who lived on the open plains and forests spanning what is now Vic and SA. The cheerful yellow flowers grew profusely in long grass in woodlands along the Yarra, Maribyrnong and Murray Rivers. Women and children dug up large numbers of tubers from the shallow soil using their wooden digging sticks.

Writing in 1852, William Buckley, the runaway convict, said *mirr-n'y-ong* was commonly eaten by the Aborigines with whom he lived for thirty years near Geelong (Vic). George Augustus Robinson (1788–1866), Chief Protector of Aborigines at Port Phillip, Melbourne, reported in 1841 that women on the open plains filled their bags and baskets with large quantities of this favourite food. 'They burn the grass,' Robinson wrote, 'the better to see these roots.'

Following the introduction of sheep, cattle and rabbits by settlers, millions of yam daisy plants were destroyed over a vast area, and with them the livelihood of the plains Aborigines. 'Indeed,' said pastoralist Edward Curr (1886), 'several thousand sheep, which I had at Colbinabbin [near Echuca], not only learnt to root up these vegetables with their noses, but they for the most part lived on them for the first year, after which the root began gradually to get scarce.' No wonder the Aborigines sometimes speared sheep!

The yam daisy is now almost extinct on the plains of western Vic.

Growing

Yam daisies adapt to most soil if it is well-drained, but produce bigger tubers in soil enriched with compost or well-rotted manure.

Growing yam daisies in bushfood gardens is still experimental, so it's probably best to start with a seedling plant, grown from an old tuber. Otherwise, sow the fresh, fluffy seeds (if you can get some) in spring. Allow 60 cm between plants.

In the wild, flowers appear in spring, but in high summer, when the weather is dry, the flowers and leaves shrivel and the old tuber becomes dormant. There is no need to water plants during this period, and in fact watering may cause tubers to rot. After the first autumn rains, a circle of new leaves sprouts above the ground and a new tuber forms below as the old one shrivels and becomes bitter. Plants exude a milky sap if any part is cut.

The tubers can be dug at any time after flowering until they start to grow again in autumn. There are varieties with large and small, smooth and misshapen tubers (like Jerusalem artichokes). Old tubers are brown (like dahlia tubers), but fresh tubers have a purple skin.

Snails attack young seedlings and new buds.

Eating

'The root is small, in taste rather sweet, not unpleasant, and perhaps more like a radish than a potato,' wrote R. Brough-Smyth in *The Aborigines of Victoria* (Melbourne, 1876). He saw yam daisies growing on the banks of Moonee Ponds near Melbourne. Aborigines washed and scraped the milky tubers and sometimes ate them uncooked. Raw tubers are crisp, with a bland, slightly bitter taste.

On the plains, women roasted the tubers in specially made rush fibre baskets in earth ovens overnight, but the baskets were often burnt and could only be used once or twice. 'When several families live near each other and cook their roots together, sometimes the baskets form a pile three feet [90 cm] high,' wrote James Dawson in *The Australian Aborigine* (Melbourne, 1886).

Yam daisy tubers contain high amounts of potassium, magnesium, sodium, calcium, iron and some zinc. Protein content is 1.5 per cent and carbohydrate content 13.3 per cent, but there is no starch, as tubers store carbohydrates as *fructosan*, which is digested by fermentation.

If baked quickly, yam daisy tubers tend to dry out and become crisp. Very low temperature slow baking will yield a treacly syrup.

The tubers can be boiled like potatoes or parsnips, served with butter and herbs, added to soups or fried as chips.

They are good steamed, cut into matchstick-sized strips and stir-fried, or battered and fried. The taste is said to have a 'spicy hot', rather than a coconut flavour.

RELATED PLANTS

Alpine yam daisy (*Microseris scapigera*)

A shorter-lived perennial, suitable for cold climate gardens. It has larger, more fibrous tubers, which are said to be less tasty than those of the common yam daisy. It is found at high altitude grasslands in Tas, the Australian Alps near Cooma, NSW, Mt Lofty, SA and in New Zealand.

CHAPTER 4

Seeds and Nuts

Seeds of life ... Ancient stone grinders found at Lake Mungo in western NSW prove that Aborigines were crushing seeds and other plant foods 15000 to 18000 years ago. In Central Australia and in the Western Desert, Aborigines made use of the edible seeds of some 75 species of grasses, acacias (wattles) and other plants. Seeds were carried about to give as gifts or to barter in exchange ceremonies. Women scattered grass seeds near soakage waters and after land was burnt.

Seed containers

Desert Aborigines had very few material possessions and carried everything they owned with them, so their tools had to have many uses.

Aboriginal women used bark or wooden dishes or containers to gather, carry and winnow edible plant seeds. These pitchis or coolamons, made of mulga or beanwood, were also used to carry babies and to dig and scrape earth. Larger dishes were shaped for carrying water balanced on the head, on a coil of hair string or grass. In northern Australia these days they are made from a car hubcap beaten flat, bent and cut to shape with tin snips.

Harvesting woollybutt grass was the frequent task of Aboriginal women in the Gibson Desert. They pulled heads of seed-bearing grass down over the dishes, then beat and winnowed them. They ground up the seeds with water into a paste which they made into cakes (*nyuma* in Pitjantjatjara), and cooked in the fire ashes.

The seed husks can be removed by rubbing them between the hands or underfoot, or by burning the grass.

In Central Australia, wet seed meal is poured into small trenches scooped in the hot coals of the campfire. The seed cake quickly forms a coat and is then covered with ash and hot sand and left to cook for 20 minutes or more.

GRASS SEEDS
Family POACEAE

On an expedition in western NSW in 1835, Major Thomas Mitchell was puzzled when he saw piles of grass, like haystacks, stretching for nine miles (about 15 km) along the Narran River near the present Lightning Ridge. We know today that the seeds from these extensive grass fields were ground between stones by Aboriginal women who shaped them into flat cakes like bread and baked them.

Travelling from SA to Darwin in the 1930s, Mr A. L. Ashwin came across an Aboriginal grain store of one tonne of seeds (probably grass seeds) stored in 17 large wooden troughs, each 1.5 m long.

Australia's native grasses, wrote Queensland's Colonial Botanist, Frederick Manson Bailey, 'sleep' through years when there is no rain, but after good rains, spring into life with fresh green herbage.

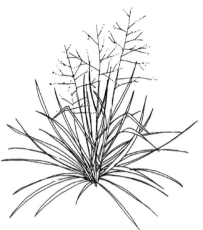

MILLET GRASS
Panicum decompositum
Aboriginal names: Cooly (Narran River, western NSW), tindal (Cloncurry River, Qld)
Other names: Australian millet, native millet, umbrella grass

CLIMATE   Arid to warm temperate
HABITAT   Common through inland Australia and the Darling Downs (Qld)
FORM   Tall, coarse, short-lived perennial bushes to 70 cm in height
FOLIAGE   Blue-green grass blades
SEEDS   Large seed heads blow about after summer rains and small, millet-like grains mature in late summer and early autumn

Growing
Like common millet, Australian millet needs little water and will grow in hot, arid places where there is a short rainy season and poor soil.

The plants are increased by seeds and spread widely after fire. Yields are heavier in cultivation. Millet seeds have a high nutrition and fibre content and are eaten by livestock.

WOOLLYBUTT GRASS
Eragrostis eriopoda
Aboriginal names: Wanganu, wangunu (Anangu, Uluru; Pintupi, NT)
Other names: Love grass, naked woollybutt

CLIMATE   Arid to warm temperate
HABITAT   Inland desert sand plains; common under mulga

FORM	Dense clumps of erect, pointy, wiry green stems 35–50 cm high with thick, white, woolly bases
SEEDS	Tiny, red-brown seeds, in summer after light rains

Woollybutt grass has long been a staple food of desert people, who gather the seeds from around ant nests. The nutritious seeds contain 13 to 17 per cent protein (more than wholemeal wheat) and large amounts of iron and zinc.

Growing
Woollybutt grows best in loose, sandy soil. It is propagated from seed.

This tough plant is drought-resistant, encouraged by fire and is eaten eagerly by livestock.

RELATED PLANTS
Many other *Eragrostis* species bear edible seeds which are used in the same way, for example, the salt-tolerant *Eragrostis falcata*, which does not have thick butts and grows on sandy soil.

Teff (*Eragrostis tef*) is the principal grain crop of Ethiopia, where it is made into a pancake bread called *ingera*.

OTHER GRASS SEEDS
Sporobulus (*Sporobolus actinocladus*)
Aboriginal name: Jil-crow-aberry (Cloncurry River, Qld)
Other names: Rat-tail grass

FAMILY POACEAE
HABITAT Top End.

'They all [Qld Aborigines] use the seeds of a small grass which grows upon pebbly ridges, called by them Jil-crow-aberry,' according to Edward Palmer in *Notes on Some Australian Tribes* (London, 1884).

The grass stalks were soaked in water to soften the seeds before grinding. Seeds are very small, but easy to collect (in late spring)

The cones, which are of enormous size, are filled with an eatable seed, much sought after by the Aborigines, who congregate in hundreds from all parts of the country during the season (that is from January to March) to feast upon them; the nuts are said to be sweet and agreeable, having an almond-like flavour ... The Bunya-bunya is found on the mountain-ranges in the district between the Brisbane and Burnett Rivers ... and the government have issued orders that ... the trees of this valuable Pine should not be cut down, or in any way injured.

George Bennett, *Gatherings of a Naturalist*, London, 1860

BUNYA NUTS

Araucaria bidwilli
Aboriginal names: Bon-yi (Turrubul, Brisbane), buhnyi (Bundjalung, northern NSW)

FAMILY	ARAUCARIA
CLIMATE	Temperate to subtropical
HABITAT	Coastal ranges and rainforest of Qld, especially the Bunya Mountains, 975–1100 altitude, near Gympie, Qld
FORM	Large, shapely, pine-like dioecious tree, 18–50 m high, spreading 10–20 m
FOLIAGE	Glossy, stiff, dark green, flat leaves, 1–5 cm long
FLOWERS	Long, stiff, pointed male catkins, 10–20 cm long
FRUITS	Woody, dark green female cones, shaped like pineapples, 20–30 cm in diameter. They contain many nuts and may weigh 4 kg
NUTS	Large, hard-shelled seeds about 2.5 cm long contain creamy white, edible kernels

Bunya or bunya bunya nuts are tasty and nutritious and the bunya pine is an imposing and shapely tree, but because of its size, is not suitable for home gardens, but is ideal for farms, large gardens and parks.

The huge trees may reach 25, 50 or even 80 m in height and take 10 years to set cones, 14 to 16 years to bear their first crop of edible nuts and 20 years before they bear well. Each pine cone, packed with perhaps 120 nuts, may weigh from 4 to 11 kg. In the season, these huge cones come crashing to the ground and can make a big dent in a car roof. The sharp, prickly branches often fall to the ground.

Surveyor John Carne Bidwill (1815–53) went to Moreton Bay to see bunya trees in the wild and brought back seeds and a living plant which he sent to Britain in 1843. However, Constance Petrie (1904) said that bunya pines were discovered by her grandfather, Scots-born Brisbane pioneer Andrew Petrie (1798–1872), who gave some specimens to Bidwell.

An avenue of bunya trees planted in 1858–67 by Colonial Botanist Walter Hill still grows along the banks of the Brisbane River in the Brisbane City Botanic Gardens.

Every three years a truce was declared between Aboriginal clans in the Blackall Ranges and more than 700 people took part in the bunya nut feasts, which were hosted by the Gubbi Gubbi, who lived between Hervey and Moreton Bays, and the Waka Waka.

Writing in 1898, Mary Bundock said the 'Richmond River Blacks' of northern NSW would travel about 200 miles (320 km) to attend bunya bunya feasts. 'Our tribe,' she wrote, 'used to come back looking very fat and well after an expedition to the Bunyas.'

A notable bunya pine in King's Avenue, Canberra, was planted on 10 May 1927 by the Duke of York. Bunyas are closely related to the recently discovered Wollemi pine of NSW.

Growing

Bunya pines, as we have emphasised, need plenty of space. They do best in deep, fertile soil, but can survive in dry places and are drought and frost tolerant. They will grow wherever citrus fruits grow.

Once trees are established, you can expect a crop each year and a bumper crop every three years.

Seed germination is slow and may take a year. Plant ripe seeds, point down, in a long, narrow pot, tube or plant bag filled with good potting soil in a sheltered spot. Before the seedlings emerge a second nut grows 2.5 cm below the seed.

Plant several trees because only female and bisexual trees bear nuts. One male tree is enough for pollination.

Repot young seedlings, which can be used as indoor plants for the next one or two years.

Before planting, prepare a hole about 60 cm deep and use a crowbar to break up the soil at the bottom of the hole to accommodate the long tap root. Water the tree and loosen soil around it with a fork.

Young plants are prickly, so livestock will leave them alone when they are planted out.

We think every Australian farm should have a grove or windbreak of bunya pines.

Eating

Bunya nuts can be left in their cones for storage as long as they are kept dry, otherwise they will go mouldy.

Raw shells are difficult to open. The best method is to boil the nuts in water for 10 to 15 minutes. While they are still hot and wet, open the shells with a sharp knife and remove the kernels. The large, oval kernels have a wonderful texture and a nutty, almost meaty taste with a slight resinous aftertaste and can be used in sweet or savoury dishes, from cream torte to meat loaves. They are a rich source of protein for vegetarians and vegans.

Fry whole bunya nuts in place of potato chips. When cool, the kernels can be minced to make nutmeat for patties and vegi-burgers or to add to bread and pastry. For a poultry or vegetable stuffing, mix equal quantities of minced bunya nuts with seasoned mashed potatoes firmed with breadcrumbs. Blend cooked bunya nuts into vegetable soups, especially pumpkin, yam or kumara. Very finely minced bunya nuts can be used as a thickener instead of cornflour.

You can roast bunya nuts in the oven or in hot ashes and then grind them finely to use as flour. It is a particularly adhesive flour and makes rich, heavy damper-like bread and interesting chappatis. Chopped bunya nuts can be used like any other nuts in desserts and cakes, especially Christmas cake. Nuts will keep for a long time stored in rum (presumably from Bundaberg!).

To make bunya nut coffee, roast bunya nuts a second time in the stove until they become quite brown. Grind finely and use as a coffee substitute.

MACADAMIA NUT

Smooth shell *Macadamia integrifolia*
Rough shell *Macadamia tetraphylla*
Aboriginal names: Boombera (NSW), kendal, kindal kindal (Qld)
Other names: Australian, baphal, bauble, bauple, bobble, bopple,
bubble or Queensland nut

FAMILY	PROTEACEAE
CLIMATE	Subtropical to warm temperate
HABITAT	Rainforests of south-eastern Qld to 400 m
FORM	Tall, smooth-trunked tree, 8–20 m tall m, spreading 4–10 m
FOLIAGE	Glossy, stiff, deep green leaves with spiny margins in whorls of three, about 20 cm long
FLOWERS	Creamy white, drooping feathery flower spikes, 25–30 cm long, spring to summer
NUTS	Shiny brown globular nuts, about 2–3 cm across, autumn and winter

Until recently, macadamia nuts were often described as 'the only Australian native plant ever developed as a commercial fruit crop'.

The smooth shelled macadamia was once common in rainforests around Mt Bauple, near Maryborough (Qld), and was called the Bauple nut. This was corrupted into 'bopple nut'. The trees were named after John Macadam, once president of the Philosophical Society of Vic. In 1858 a specimen of *Macadamia integrifolia* was brought from the bush near Gympie (Qld), and planted in the Brisbane City Botanic Gardens.

In 1927 Parramatta nurseryman Herbert J. Ramsey filled an order from the United States Department of Agriculture for 10,000 macadamia nut seeds. Cross breeding in Hawaii produced nuts with softer shells.

RELATED PLANTS

Bush nut (*Macadamia tetraphylla*)
This is the rough-shelled macadamia nut, which is found in similar country to M. *integrifolia*. There are natural hybrids of the two species where these areas meet. The hard shells are sometimes pointed and have a rough surface. Trees reach 20 m in height and bear slightly oval nuts about 2.5 cm long, which mature from March to July.

Growing

A high summer rainfall area, rich, moist soil and a large garden are needed to grow macadamia trees successfully. They are more cold-hardy than avocadoes and can be raised in warm temperate climate given irrigation or regular watering in summer and some dry spells.

Macadamia nuts thrive in coastal areas of high humidity, with light or few frosts. They will yield a good crop in Sydney and further south. They require frequent watering and protection from wind but are heat and cold tolerant once established. The trees will grow on a wide range of soils, but like a deep, rich, moist soil, which can be acid. Propagate from grafted seedlings and transplant when 45 cm tall, spacing 9 to 10 m apart.

Plant in full sun to semi-shade. The seeds germinate in about 30 to 60 days.

Grafted trees will bear nuts in four or five years, but seedlings may take 10 years to come into bearing. A mature grafted tree will yield 50 kg of in-shell nuts.

The major commercial growing area is around Lismore and Mullumbimby in northern NSW. Macadamias also do well around Perth, particularly on the heavy clay soils along the Swan River, and as far north as Carnarvon, where grafted trees bear at six years of age and 10 year old trees yield 10 to 13 kg of nuts per tree from January to August.

Eating

Macadamia nuts are delicious, but have very hard shells, which need a special nut cracker or gentle persuasion with a vice or hammer to crack open. They crack more easily when frozen. If left on the tree, the leather husk opens, the nuts drop out and can be collected from the ground.

The nuts are free of cholesterol, rich in mono-unsaturated oils, vitamins and minerals. Their oil content (78 per cent) is the highest of any type of nut.

Macadamia nuts may be eaten raw, roasted, deep fried or dried. Roasted nuts can be mixed with drier nuts like almonds and put through a grinder to make a nutritious paste rather like peanut butter. The nuts can be coated with chocolate and made into spreads, sauces, ice cream and fudge. Macadamia oil, used as a cooking oil or for salads, has a slightly sweet taste.

Muffins

Basic mix

2 ½ cups self raising flour

½ teaspoon baking powder

¾ cup caster sugar

2 eggs, lightly beaten

1 cup milk

50 ml vegetable oil or melted butter

Flavourings

• 1 to 2 cups chopped bushfruits

• Or, 3 tablespoons wattleseed

• Or, replace ¼ cup milk with wattleseed essence

• Or, ¼ cup finely chopped macadamia or bunya nuts

Topping

Finely chopped macadamia or other nuts

Grease a muffin tray with oil spray or butter.

Sift flour, baking powder and sugar into a bowl.

Stir in eggs, milk and oil (or butter) and mix well. Stir in your chosen flavouring and spoon the mix into the prepared muffin tray.

Sprinkle with nuts and bake in a hot (210°C) oven for about 25 minutes.

Muffins are best served warm straight from the oven, but they'll keep one to two days if stored in a cake tin.

Wattleseed: the new flavour of Australia

The intriguing taste of wattleseed, somewhere between coffee and chocolate with a hint of vanilla, appeals to our palates. Wattleseed can be used to flavour drinks, coffee, bread, biscuits, cakes, muffins, tortes, sauces and ice cream, mousse, parfait and pancakes.

We believe this unique food crop will become a part of everyday eating here and all around the world.

Acacias or wattles produce pods which contain protein-rich hard-coated seeds. These seeds are roasted and used whole, ground into a fine powder or made into an essence.

Wattleseed is nutritious. It contains 17 to 25 per cent protein, 4 to 16 per cent fat and 26 to 40 per cent carbohydrate, depending on the species. It is the major commercial crop of the Australian bushfoods industry, with 7.5 to 10 tonnes of wattleseed already being produced and sold annually.

WATTLES
FAMILY MIMOSACEAE

Wattles or acacias are trees or shrubs which bear profuse yellow or creamy ball or spike blossoms and are found in most climatic zones of Australia.

There are more than 500 species—the largest group of flowering plants in Australia. About 130 species grow in the vast arid zone of Central Australia, the majority growing south of Alice Springs.

So far, only about 50 species of wattles are known to produce seeds which are safe to eat. The big three are prickly wattle or gundabluey, mulga and witjuti (witchetty) bush. There are a few species which are toxic and many have unpalatable seeds.

Acacias are classed as *xerophytes*, or 'dry living' plants. This means that to conserve moisture they have developed tough, flattened or needle-like stems called *phyllodes*, which look like true leaves and do the same work. Trees and shrubs have long taproots and root systems and their root nodules 'fix' atmospheric nitrogen into the earth. Seeds regenerate after bushfires or long droughts.

Each wattle seed has a tail-like *aril* attached to it. These are protein rich and sometimes brightly coloured. They also contribute to the taste of the seeds and can be eaten raw as a snack. Ants collect the seeds.

Acacias grow rapidly and produce high yields in arid climates, so many kinds are being trialled in the sub-Sahara Sahel region of Africa and other dry places. Acacias are also found in America, Asia, Africa and Europe, where they are called mimosas.

Preparing Wattleseed

The edible seeds of several kinds of wattles are part of the traditional diet of Aborigines, especially those living in the semi-arid centre of Australia. This is how the Anangu near Uluru (Ayers Rock) prepare mulga seeds.

They collect pods of hard, mature wattleseed, or spread branches with immature pods over bark or canvas and leave them to dry on the ground under the tree. They separate seeds from the pods by rubbing and tapping them or treading them underfoot.

Yandying

The cleaned seeds are parched in hot sand and ashes to make the hard cases crack open. The women then 'yandy' or winnow the seeds to separate them from chaff, dirt, ash and fire coals by rhythmic shaking and rocking in a bark coolamon or pitchi. Pitjantjatjara women complain that yandying prickly wattle makes them cough and choke.

Roasted seeds were ground by a small, smooth grinding stone, which women carried with them and then made into a paste with water. This paste was made into little cakes which were then baked.

Wattle trees provide firewood, building material (wattle and daub), timber for digging sticks, fodder and honey. In the past, they have been utilised for tanning, making perfume, and as fuel and windbreaks.

Growing

Acacias grow quickly, but most have a short life span.

They adapt to a wide range of climates and soil conditions, from the arid inland to coastal swamps. Wattle seeds must be treated to enable them to germinate. The plants can also be propagated from cuttings. See **Chapter 6, Growing Bushfoods, p.118.**

Plant the treated seeds where they are to grow or in pots and transplant them as soon as the seed leaves open. The long taproots develop quickly and are easily damaged. Pinch back tip growth to bush out the tree.

Eating

Wattles are easy to grow, but gathering, treating and preparing the seeds is complicated and time-consuming. Pods must be picked, dried and opened to obtain the seeds, which, in turn, must be dried, cleaned and then steamed or roasted.

You can buy prepared, roasted wattleseed in packets. The fairly high price reflects the number of processes which have taken place. The wattleseed flavour is quite strong, so you only need to use small quantities.

The green seed pods of some wattle species can be eaten raw or cooked in fire ashes. The lazy way is to throw branches laden with young, green pods over a grass fire; the heat steams opens the pods, so the seeds can be removed easily. Seeds of some wattle species can be collected and processed when green, but it's easier if they are mdark brown and dry.

Wattleseed is good lightly toasted in a dry, cast-iron frypan.

Flavouring with Wattleseed Essence
Wattleseed has the consistency of rough coffee grounds, and can be used in this form in baking. For a smoother texture, however, make wattleseed essence.

Wattleseed Essence
1 cup water
2–3 tablespoons ground wattleseed
Bring water to the boil, stir in the seeds and keep boiling for 5 to 6 minutes, stirring now and again. Strain, and allow to cool.
The discarded seeds can be added to bread, biscuits and cakes.
The resulting essence can be stored in a container in the refrigerator for up to two weeks.

Wattleseed 'Coffee'
Take about 1/4 cup hot wattleseed essence.
Top up with boiling water and add sugar to taste.
In the bush, take 4 heaped teaspoons of crushed wattleseed, roast them in a pan over the fire and pour in water.

Easy Wattleseed Ice Cream
Slightly soften vanilla ice cream.
Mix in wattleseed essence and refreeze.

COASTAL WATTLE

Acacia longifolia var. *sophorae* (syn. *Acacia sophorae*)
Aboriginal names: Boobialla, boobyalla (Tas)
Other names: Coast wattle, golden wattle

CLIMATE	Temperate
HABITAT	Coastal sands behind beaches in SE Australia, from Qld to SA and Tas
FORM	Dense, sprawling shrub 3–5 m tall, spreading 3–6 m
FOLIAGE	Short, broad, leathery, curved, dark green phyllodes, 5–10 cm long
FLOWERS	Profuse golden spikes, in spring
PODS	Cylindrical, straight or slightly curved and beaked brown pods, 5–10 cm long
SEEDS	Large seeds are retained in the pod and ripen in summer

Growing

Coastal wattle tolerates salt and harsh seaside conditions and thrives in high rainfall areas.

The plants grow quickly. They are used to stabilise sand dunes, and grow into a dense shrub if protected from wind. Sprawling branches take root wherever they are covered by soil or sand.

Eating

The large, protein-rich seeds have a bitter, sulphurous taste when raw and are best eaten after roasting or steaming the green pods. Roasted seeds give a pleasant nutty flavour to pancakes, bread and cakes. A coffee substitute is made from the roasted seeds.

GOLDEN WATTLE

Acacia pycnantha
Other names: Green, broad-leaved or South Australian wattle

CLIMATE	Temperate to semi-arid
HABITAT	Dry eucalypt forests of inland NSW, ACT, Vic and SA
FORM	Small tree, 3–6 m high, spreading 3–5 m
FOLIAGE	Curved, broad, shiny, deep green phyllodes, 18 cm long

FLOWERS	Large, perfumed golden balls in early spring
PODS	Broad, straight pods, 5–12 cm long, open and drop seeds to the ground, which are dispersed by ants
SEEDS	Moderate sized oval seeds with a small aril are shed from pods

The ornamental golden wattle, the largest flowering wattle, is the floral emblem of Australia. It has been cultivated for many years for its bark, which is rich in tannic acid. The dried leaves are also a good source of tannin for curing leather. Perfume is extracted from the aromatic flowers.

Growing
Golden wattle is a dependable seed producer, even in drought years.

The trees grow quickly, but only live from 5 to 15 years and should be replanted every few years. They adapt to a wide range of soil and will grow in clay, sand or poor, stony, dry or shallow soils. They do best, of course, in well-drained soil with adequate water, but not at high altitudes or in very wet conditions. They regenerate naturally.

MULGA
Acacia aneura
Aboriginal names: Mandja, manya, wardiji (Warlpiri, NT), mulga (Central Australia), wintalyka (Anangu, Uluru, NT), yarran (Vic). The seeds: Ititya (Arrernte, NT)
Other names: Desert mulga

CLIMATE	Arid to warm temperate
HABITAT	Widespread on sand plains and sandhills through inland Australia (except Vic)
FORM	A 6–7 m tall woody shrub or small tree, often much-branched
FOLIAGE	Long, needle-like phyllodes, 3–10 cm long
FLOWERS	Short spikes of 3 cm long cylindrical yellow flower-heads, usually in spring after rains
PODS	Broad, 2.5 cm long flat pods, grey-green to brown, papery to wooden
SEEDS	Small, glossy, dark brown, oval seeds, 3–5 per pod, ripe spring and summer

Mulga is an important, and widely used tree of Central Australia. Desert Aborigines used the heartwood to make digging sticks and shields, spear shafts and clubs (nulla-nullas) and, these days, for a range of souvenirs for tourists.

Growing

Mulga is a slow growing, but long-lived tree which is drought and fire resistant. The trees tolerate a wide range of soils, including lime and heavy clay, but need good drainage.

If you have enough space, plant mulga in groups in association with wijuti bush (*Acacia kempeana*), just as they grow in the wild.

Mulga makes a good shade tree for the hot, dry inland. The leaves are eaten by livestock, especially sheep.

RELATED PLANTS

There are several mulga varieties, notably *Acacia aneura* var. *conifera*, which has horizontal branches like a fir tree and grows to 10 m in height.

PRICKLY WATTLE (GUNDABLUEY)

Acacia victoriae (syn. *Acacia sentis*)
Aboriginal names: Ariepe (Arrernte, NT), ganabargu (Warlpiri, NT), ngatunpa (Pitjatjantjara, NT), pulkuru (Pintupi, NT), waliputa (Murchison, WA). The seeds: Ntange ariepe (Arrernte, NT)
Other names: Bramble wattle, elegant wattle, gundabluey

CLIMATE	Semi-arid to warm temperate
HABITAT	Open scrub, rocky hillsides and grasslands of semi-arid areas
FORM	Much-branched shrub or small tree, 2–5 m high, with spiny thorns along branches
FOLIAGE	Dense, bright blue-green foliage, with narrow, broad or sickle-shaped phyllodes, 2–5 cm long
FLOWERS	Pale yellow balls, alone or in pairs, in spring–summer
PODS	Masses of thin, papery, flat yellow-green seed pods, 4–8 cm long, turning light brown when mature in summer
SEEDS	Pods contain 4–6 oval, grape-sized brown seeds with small arils

Prickly wattles have been planted to harvest for wattleseed on a commercial scale in the Flinders Ranges (SA). They also grow successfully in Iran, Israel and Pakistan. The botanical name *Acacia victoriae* refers to the Victoria River (Qld).

Growing
Prickly wattles grow wild in dry or stony inland areas, where they often indicate the presence of nearby water. Their roots plunge as much as 24 to 27 m deep beneath the earth. Trees are frost hardy and grow fairly quickly, flowering in two years, and bear a heavy and uniform seed crop. They will grow in exposed, sunny places and make good low windbreaks.

RELATED PLANTS
Acacia victoriae subsp. *arida* is found in drier western areas including the Simpson Desert.

WIJUTI BUSH
Acacia kempeana (syn. *Acacia sibirica*)
Aboriginal names: Atnyeme (Arrernte, NT), ilykuwara (Anangu, Uluru, NT), galgiri, ngalkirdi (Warlpiri, NT)
Other names: Kempe's wattle, witchetty bush

CLIMATE	Semi-arid to arid
HABITAT	Dry, inland areas of all mainland states except Vic
FORM	Grey-green shrub, 2–3 m tall, spreading 3 m, or single-trunked tree to 5 m
FOLIAGE	Smooth, elongated, blunt-tipped phyllodes (sticky when young), 3–10 cm long
FLOWERS	Golden yellow cylindrical spike flowers, 2–4 cm long in spring for a long period

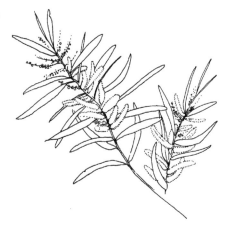

| PODS | Brown, oblong, flat pods, 3–5 cm long |
| SEEDS | Small, black, oval-shaped with a small aril |

Witchetty grubs are found in the roots of this tree. It is named for the Rev. A. H. Kempe (1844–1928), one of the Lutheran missionaries at Hermannsburg (NT). In 1877 he collected specimens on the Finke River.

Eat the Flowers

Flowers of the white sallow or 'sally' wattle (*Acacia floribunda*), green wattle (*Acacia decurrens*) and most other wattle species can be eaten safely.

Add the fluffy little flower heads, without stalks, to pancakes, scones, scrambled eggs and omelettes. Try only a few the first time, in case you might be allergic to them.

CHAPTER 5

Nectar Plants

Sweet drinks   Many of Australia's spectacular colourful flowering plants produce a sweet, honey-like solution of sugars called nectar. Bees make honey from it by reducing its water content. Like the bees, Aborigines suck the sweet liquid as they pass by, or collect blossoms to soak in water to make sweet (and even alcoholic) drinks.

BANKSIA
FAMILY PROTEACEAE

There are about 73 species of banksias and the great majority—58 of them—are native to the SW corner of WA.

They bear spectacular cylindrical flower spikes, which are a source of nectar for bees, birds and possums and make lovely cut flowers.

Aborigines suck the liquid from the flowers on the tree or shake out nectar against their hands. They soak the flower spikes in water to make a sweet drink, which is sometimes mixed with wattle gum. A weak form of alcohol, once called 'bool' or 'bull', is produced if the liquid is left to ferment.

Botanist George Caley, who collected plants in NSW for Sir Joseph Banks, was intrigued by a group of Aborigines at a waterfall on the Cataract River (previously named after his Aboriginal guide Moowattin), near Appin, west of Sydney.

Caley watched as the men collected spiky banksia flowerheads and steeped them in water, which they afterwards drank. 'As I well knew the natives prefer sweetness in a greater degree than Europeans, it immediately occurred to my mind, that this liquor on being fermented would become an agreeable beverage,' Caley told Banks in a letter written in October 1807. He said the Aborigines had been using *Banksia spinulosa*, which they called *ing'ra* or *ingera*, adding: 'I have heard that different tribes assemble frequently when *ingera* is abundant, purposely to drink it, which may be truly called a native feast.'

Collecting vegetable plants was women's work among the Nyunga of WA, except for the honey flowers of the banksia. Ethnologist Mrs Daisy Bates noted that 'the women receive but a very little portion, the honey being a favourite food of the natives [men]'.

Growing
In the wild, most banksias grow in poor, sandy soils.

Banksias store their seeds in woody capsules, which may stay closed for long periods, although the coast banksia (*Banksia integrifolia*) spits out its seeds quite suddenly.

The seeds do not require any special treatment. Fresh from the cones, they will germinate in a few weeks. If the trees are burnt by bushfire or the cones break, the seeds fall to the ground and germinate after the first rain.

Sow one or two seeds in pots. The seedlings are prone to damping-off.

> **Nectar Blossom Cordial**
>
> Pick banksia and other nectar plant flowers early in the morning, while they are still laden with sticky nectar.
>
> Soak the blossoms for a few hours in cold water out of the sun (to stop them fermenting) or in the refrigerator.
>
> This cordial drink is delicious and contains vitamin C and minerals. It can also be used to make an unusual jelly.

BULL BANKSIA

Banksia grandis
Aboriginal names: Boollgalla, bungkara, poolgarla (Nyungar, WA). The drink: Mangite, mangkatj, mungitch (Nyungar, WA)

CLIMATE	Temperate
HABITAT	Jarrah forests and coastal tuart woodlands of SW Australia
FORM	Shrub to 1.5 m, spreading 3 m, or much-branched tree to 10 m
FOLIAGE	Large, triangular-lobed dark green leaves along a central spine
FLOWERS	Large, pale yellow flower spikes 30–40 cm long and 8 cm in diameter, spring to midsummer

The attractive leaves and flower spikes of this species are the largest of any banksias. 'The natives gather the flowers and extract a sweet juice resembling honey,' wrote Lieutenant Richard Dale at King George Sound (now Albany) in 1843.

Growing
Bull banksia grows best in a sunny spot in deep, sandy soil, but will grow in mountain areas over limestone. Propagate from seed.

The trees thrive where there are moist winters and mild summers. They are difficult to grow in the eastern states.

COAST BANKSIA

Banksia integrifolia
Aboriginal names: Courriddjah (Dharug, western Sydney), pomera (Qld)

Other names: Beefwood, coastal honeysuckle, golden bottlebrush

CLIMATE   Temperate
HABITAT   Seashore and coastal areas of Qld, NSW and Vic
FORM   Small to large woody tree, 3–6 m high, with a gnarled trunk
FOLIAGE   Short, narrow dark green leaves, silver-grey on the underside
FLOWERS   Yellow-lemon or yellow-bronze spikes 7–15 cm long, with
           a pleasant aroma, all year

Coast banksia has unusual, woody cones, which attract birds and bees.
Prostrate form grows only 2 m high.

Growing

Unlike most other banksias, seeds of coast banksia spring out of the
capsules, so watch out for them. Trees are hardy and withstand harsh
coastal conditions.

HAIRPIN BANKSIA
Banksia spinulosa
Aboriginal names: Ing'ra, ingera (Dharug, Appin area, NSW)
Other names: Golden banksia

CLIMATE   Temperate
HABITAT   Open forests of eastern Vic to NSW and Qld
FORM   Bushy shrub or small tree, 1–3 m high
FOLIAGE   Long, narrow serrated leaves 2–8 cm long
FLOWERS   Cylindrical flower spikes, pale lemon, golden or bronze,
           5–20 cm long with rows of rigid, bent, wiry, black, golden,
           orange or red styles ('hairpins'), all year

Heads of the hairpin banksia are filled with sticky nectar which lures
New Holland honeyeaters to feast on them. Seeds are a woody sac in the
cone of withered flowers.

Growing

Hairpin banksia will survive on the coast or the mountains, in open sun or
semi-shade and even in damp spots. Plants resist salt spray and are hardy if

planted in well-drained light to medium soil, where there is plenty of moisture.

Propagate from seed or tip cuttings. The trees have a lignotuber or swelling at the base of the stem.

RELATED PLANTS

There are many forms of hairpin banksia. A dwarf species flowers in winter.

Hill banksia (*Banksia spinulosa* var. *collin*) has deep-golden flowers and fine, serrated leaves, but does not develop a lignotuber.

B. spinulosa 'Birthday Candles', a late-flowering cultivar developed and introduced by Austraflora Nurseries of Melbourne, can be grown in pots or small gardens.

SAW BANKSIA
Banksia serrata
Aboriginal names: Watangal, wattangarry (Eora, Sydney), wattungurree (Dharug, western Sydney)
Other names: Old Man banksia, red honeysuckle

CLIMATE	Temperate
HABITAT	Open forest, sand dunes and sandy regions of coastal NSW, Vic and Tas
FORM	Small to medium tree, often with twisted, gnarled trunks and dark grey, pebbly bark when mature, reaching 6–10 m.
FOLIAGE	Serrated, thick, glossy, flat, deep green leaves, 7.5–15 cm long, paler and hairy on the underside; new growth is red-brown
FLOWERS	Open as blue-grey buds and become large, erect golden cylindrical bottlebrush spikes, 15 cm x 10 cm, which dry to bronze, in summer (best in alternate years)

Banksia serrata was named by Carl Linnaeus the Younger in honour of Sir Joseph Banks (1743–1820), who collected plants at Botany Bay in

April 1770 and took them to England. The actual specimen collected by Banks is in the National Herbarium in Melbourne. Banksias were listed for sale by the Kensington (London) nurserymen Lee and Kennedy in 1788.

These twisted, gnarled trees, with their sharp, sawtooth leaves and grotesque bristly old cones, were the model for the big, bad Banksia Man in Australian author May Gibbs's *Snugglepot and Cuddlepie* stories.

They are a valuable source of food for possums, which fertilise the flowers as they lick off nectar. They are also pollinated by honeysuckers.

Growing

Saw banksias thrive in poor sandy soil. They should have a well-drained spot in the garden, where they will form a smaller tree. These hardy trees survive bushfires.

RELATED PLANTS

B. serrata 'Austraflora pygmy possum' is a tiny, prostrate hybrid, spreading to 30 cm.

TROPICAL BANKSIA

Banksia dentata
Aboriginal name: Miyu (Jaywon, Katherine, NT)
Other names: Swamp banksia

CLIMATE	Tropical
HABITAT	Moist areas and sandy soils of northern Australia
FORM	Small, rough-barked tree, 5–7 m in height
FOLIAGE	Narrow, toothed green leaves, white and hairy on the underside
FLOWERS	Cream to pale yellow cylindrical spike flowers to 13 cm long, in summer and autumn

Nectar flows copiously from the blossoms of the tropical banksia. On Groote Eylandt, Aboriginal women pick the blossoms early in the morning, hit them against a coolamon or their hands and lick up the nectar. Blossoms are also soaked in water.

The old flower spikes are used to carry fire and also act as hair brushes.

CALLISTEMON
FAMILY MYRTACEAE

The name 'bottlebrush' is usually given to plants of the Callistemon species, hardy shrubs or small trees which have flowers arranged in dense cylindrical spikes or brushes.

The flower colours include red, pink, whites, yellow and mauve. There are about 20 species, all native to Australia.

Growing
Callistemons tolerate poor, salty soils and adapt to wet or dry conditions, but don't transplant easily. The plants grow readily from mature seed, that is, from seed capsules which are at least three years old. In the wild the woody capsules may not open for several years.

The tiny seeds, as small as particles of dust, should be mixed with sand before sowing. You can also strike new plants from cuttings taken after new growth starts to harden in late summer.

Callistemons in the wild grow along creeks, so they need plenty of water. Prune spent flowers to encourage new flowers and to stop bushes becoming straggly and woody.

Callistemons are often planted as park and street trees.

Drinking
The flowers are sucked for their nectar or made into a sweet, pleasant drink (see **Banksia,** p.104).

CRIMSON BOTTLEBRUSH
Callistemon citrinus
Other names: Lemon bottlebrush

CLIMATE	Temperate to tropical
HABITAT	Damp, sandy flats of SE Australia
FORM	Bushy shrub or small tree, 2–4 m high and 2 m wide with arched branches
FOLIAGE	Stiff, flat, pointed, lance-shaped lemon-scented leaves, 3–8 cm long
FLOWERS	Red bottlebrush spikes, 5–12 cm long, with purple anthers, spring and early summer

RELATED PLANTS

Alpine bottlebrush (*Callistemon sieberi*)
A rounded, woody shrub (to 2 m) with fine needle leaves, growing near creeks in cool temperate low altitude areas of SE Australia. Small clusters of short, pale lemon spikes flower in summer.

Weeping bottlebrush (*Callistemon viminalis*)
A weeping large shrub or tree, 5 to 6 m high, spreading 5 m, bearing bright red flower spikes in early summer and autumn.
Habitat: NSW and Vic. *C. viminalis* 'Captain Cook' has a willowy, drooping habit, and grows 1.5 to 2.5 m high and 2 m wide with rich red flowers in spring.
Habitat: Coast and mountains.

CIDER GUM

Eucalyptus gunnii
Other names: Cider tree, sugar gum, swamp gum, white gum

FAMILY	EUCALYPTUS
CLIMATE	Cool temperate
HABITAT	Tasmanian mountains 600–1100 m in snow and in high places of SE Australia, from SA to Berrima (NSW)
FORM	Tall, straight, smooth-barked perennial tree, growing to 15–20 m
FOLIAGE	Rounded, blue-grey or silver-grey young leaves, maturing to 5–7 cm long and 2–3 cm wide
FLOWERS	White flowers in summer
SYRUP	Sap flows from the trees in spring

In the cool northern areas of the United States, settlers copied the native Americans, who tapped maple trees to collect the flowing liquid 'sugar'. Farmers today say maple syrup is as good as money in the bank.

The syrup from the Tasmanian cider gum, which Aborigines used to tap, may turn out to be just as valuable in Australia.

Growing

The cider gum is a fast-growing, tall, straight tree, with smooth, grey-pink bark. It thrives in cool areas and at high altitudes. The trees thrive in well-drained soils, but adapt well to moist or heavy ones and even to drier inland districts if regularly watered.

They are slow-growing, but cold, frost and snow hardy and grow successfully in the northern hemisphere, for example at Kew Gardens in London, UK and at Wester Ross in Scotland.

Cider gums are widely admired for their pretty, rounded silver-grey juvenile foliage, which is used by florists as a contrast to cut flowers. This is a good shade tree for cool places and the sweet leaves are enjoyed by farm livestock.

Sipping cider

Tasmanian Aborigines used to bore holes through the bark of the sugar gum to tap the sweet, honey-coloured, sugary sap. The liquid trickled down the trunk and was collected at the base of the tree.

Early settlers cut holes in the tree trunk, large enough to hold one pint (600 mL). The cavity filled daily and the liquid was drunk straight away.

If left to stand, wild yeasts cause fermentation and the sap becomes alcoholic. 'At Christmas time, in 1826, the Lake Arthur [Tas] blacks indulged in a great eucalyptus cider orgy,' according to Dr John McPherson.

When stored in capped glass bottles, cider gum syrup ferments and effervesces naturally. The liquid tastes and smells just like apple cider.

Cider gum will soon come onto the market in one form or another. Gil and Meredith Freeman of Tarnuk Bushfoods planted a grove of 500 cider gum trees in 1988, and expect to start tapping about 2000.

DRYANDRA
FAMILY   PROTEACEAE

Dryandra blossoms produce quantities of strong, sweet, honey-smelling nectar over a long period. Several species, known as 'honeypots', are favourites of beekeepers.

Dryandras are closely related to banksias, but have wide, rather than long cone, flowerheads. There are about 80 known species. They now grow only in a small section of SW Australia. Dryandras were once wide-spread and fossil plants millions of years old have been found in brown coal deposits in Victoria.

There is a wide variety of forms and colours. Some are prostrate shrubs, others are small trees with prickly leaves in all shapes and sizes and shiny yellow, gold, bronze or orange rounded flowerheads.

Dryandras were collected by Archibald Menzies (1754–1842) botanist aboard the sloop HMS *Discovery* in 1791 at King George's Sound (Albany). They were named in 1810 by botanist Robert Brown after the Swedish botanist Jonas Dryander (d. 1810), a curator in Sir Joseph Banks' library. The seeds were taken to the Royal Botanic Gardens at Kew and were first sold in English nurseries in 1827.

Later, several Dryandra species were collected by botanist James Drummond (1784–1863) of Hawthornden (WA). He spent 20 years exploring the extreme south-west of the state.

Caution

Make sure you wear thick gloves when you pick dryandra flowerheads as masses of prickly leaves tightly enclose them.

Hakea blossom needles are also dangerously sharp.

Growing

Gardeners in Australia's eastern states have tried, but with only limited success, to raise plants of this unique WA genus. All too often, plants develop the fungus *Phyptophthora cinnamomi*. One way around this problem is to graft dryandras onto a resistant rootstock, such as banksia. Some dryandras are now growing reliably in Melbourne and other parts of Victoria.

Well-drained sandy or gravelly soil is best, though some dryandras grow wild in swamps.

A layer of crushed limestone or ground-up limestone chips dug into the soil 10 to 30 cm deep will reproduce their natural habitat. Dig iron chelates into the soil around them if the foliage turns yellow.

Dryandras grow in full sun or under taller plants and should be sheltered from winds. They resist frost and drought.

Most dryandras shed their seeds annually. Propagate from fresh seed in late summer or early autumn, using a potting mix made up of three parts of coarse sand to one part each of peat moss and garden soil. The seeds germinate in 3 to 6 weeks. Cuttings are difficult to strike.

Dryandras tend to become top-heavy in cultivation and benefit from light pruning after flowering.

RELATED PLANTS
Parrot bush (*Dryandra sessilis*)
Aboriginal name: Pudjak (Nyungar, WA)
Other names: Holly-leaf dryandra

Domed yellow flowers, 3 cm long, bloom from winter to spring and after rain. A shrub or small tree (3 to 6 m tall), common in temperate climate thickets through coastal limestone and jarrah plains of SW Australia. The sharp, prickly toothed, fan-shaped grey-green leaves reach 5 cm long.

Prostrate Dryandra species include *Dryandra nivea* and *D. pteridifolia*. *D. tenuifolia* is a sprawling plant with erect, toothed leaves and heads of dark brown flowers.

GREVILLEAS
FAMILY PROTEACEAE

Grevilleas or 'spider flowers' were named after Charles F. Greville (1749–1809), a founder of the British Horticultural Society. There are about 250 Australian species, the majority in SW Australia.

Most species prefer acid soils, but they will adapt to most soils except poorly drained sandy ones. Regular pruning prolongs the life and flowering period of these evergreen shrubs.

DESERT GREVILLEA
Grevillea juncifolia
Aboriginal name: Kaliny-kalinypa (Anangu, Uluru, NT), Ultukunpa (Pitjantjatjara, NT), walunari (Warlpiri, NT)
Other names: Honey grevillea, honeysuckle grevillea

CLIMATE   Semi-arid to warm temperate
HABITAT   Red sandhills and sandy spinifex plains of Central Australia

FORM	Spreading shrub with fibrous bark, to 4 m tall and 2.5 m
FOLIAGE	Narrow, pointed, green-silver needle leaves, 12–25 cm long
FLOWERS	Tapering, cylindrical, bright orange-yellow flower spikes, 8–16 cm long, after rain in spring and summer
FRUITS	Clustered pods, slightly hairy and rounded with a small spike; pods have papery winged seeds

Large, conspicuous flowers contain sticky golden nectar or 'sweet honey'. They are pollinated by honeyeaters and other birds, which get 'drunk' if the nectar ferments.

Drinking

The long, orange blossoms of desert grevillea are an abundant source of golden nectar, which can be sucked from the flowers on the tree.

For a sweet, dark drink (called *wama* by the Anangu at Uluru, NT), soak the blossoms in water and squeeze them by hand. The sweet taste 'goes off' if the brew is left to stand.

When nectar flows were copious (about once every 10 years) Aboriginal men used to make alcoholic drinks by steeping the blossoms in water.

RELATED PLANTS

Honey grevillea (*Grevillea eriostachya*)
Other names: Flame grevillea, inland flame, orange grevillea

A beautiful grevillea from the sandy deserts and heaths of SW Australia, with dense, sticky, pale-orange flower spikes which yield golden nectar. The shrubs reach 1 to 2 m high. The blossoms form after rain.

HAKEA
FAMILY PROTEACEA

The honey-like nectar exuding from the blossoms of some hakea species is often so abundant that it flows along the branches and covers the twigs.

When pressing hakea blossoms for herbarium specimens in the 1880s, William Bauerlen, a plant collector for botanist Joseph Maiden and the NSW Technological Museum in Ultimo (Sydney), was startled when the thick, rich brown nectar ran out between the papers.

There are about 120 species of hakea, all indigenous to Australia, about 80 of them to SW WA.

Some species have stiff, flat, broad, leathery leaves with toothed margins, while those growing in arid places have thin,cylindrical,sharply-pointed leaves which are a defence against the hot desert sun. They are called needle bushes.

Hakeas are named after the German botanical patron, Baron von Hake (1745–1818).

The woody fruit pods split in half, each containing two winged seeds. Seed capsules or fruits are big, hard and knobbly. Some are shaped like bird beaks, others are covered with ridges, sharp points, warty lumps or growths like pieces of cork,and a few are large and flat.

Some hakeas give off a heavy, almost overpowering fragrance.

Growing

Hakeas will grow in all Australian climates (except cold ones) and in most soils (except clay). Plants are slightly frost-tender when young.

A sunny, well-drained spot and moderate rainfall is essential to promote flower and nectar production.

The seeds are retained in the capsules, which often stay on the plants until they are burnt off by bushfires. Propagate new plants from seed. The hard-coated seeds should be pre-treated, by immersing them in near-boiling water or by nicking or filing the seed. Otherwise strike cuttings of half-ripened wood.

The seedlings regenerate readily after fire. When planting trees stake them firmly, as they can easily be uprooted by strong winds.

Drinking

To make a sweet, dark cordial drink, soak hakea blossoms in a coolamon or other container of water and squeeze them out. When the weather is very hot, Pitjanjatjara women sip this strong drink slowly through a dry grass dipped in the liquid.

CORKWOOD HAKEA

Hakea suberea (syn. *Hakea lorea*)
Aboriginal names: Biriwa (Walpiri, NT) witintji, witjinti (Pitjantjatjara, NT)

CLIMATE	Semi-arid to warm temperate
HABITAT	Widespread through mulga plains of northern inland Australia
FORM	Gnarled tree 4–5 m high with corky, fissured bark
FOLIAGE	Long, dark green needles 30 cm long
FLOWERS	Grevillea-like pale-yellow flowers in dense clusters

Droplets of dark nectar drip from sweet, sugary crystals on hanging corkwood hakea blossoms. Flowers can be collected in a coolamon and soaked in water to make a drink.

A Central Australian creation story tells how the Kandi-Tjukurapa (corkwood tree sisters) camped at Walpa Gorge to collect blossoms. At this totemic site, rock features in the landscape represent the sisters, their coolamons and flat stones, their grinding stones and the rock waterholes.

Most hakeas retain seeds in their mature woody fruits, but corkwood capsules open to shed the seeds.

RELATED PLANTS
Another corkwood (*Hakea divaricata*) has shorter, forked leaves. It flowers in winter and spring in central Australia on ranges, rocky areas and hills.

NEEDLEWOOD HAKEA
Hakea leucoptera
Aboriginal name: Ilpeye (Arrernte, NT)
Other names: Needlewood bush, silver needlewood

CLIMATE	Semi-arid to warm temperate
HABITAT	Inland Australia, including the Central Desert, on poor, sandy soils
FORM	Erect or spreading shrub, to 3–4 m
FOLIAGE	Sharp, needle-like 3–7 cm long leaves protect the flowers

FLOWERS   Fuzzy, spidery white flowers, like tangled threads, in
            clusters, spring and summer

Needlewood flowers are prized for their nectar in the Central Desert, where
Aborigines obtain good drinking water from the roots of the shrub.

Growing
Propagate needlebush hakea from the seeds. They have pale coloured
wings unlike those of other hakea which are black. The plants are hardy
and like dry areas and hot, dry summers. They will thrive in sandy soil
and help to prevent erosion. When pruned they make good fence, hedge
or screen plants. The needles deter livestock.

RELATED PLANTS
Broad-leaved sea-urchin (*Hakea petiolaris*)
A dense, spreading tree, 3 to 5 m tall, with stiff, silver-grey leaves, 5 to 10 cm
long, and striking globular crimson purple 'pincushions' with lemon yellow
'pins', 4 to 5 cm across, in late spring. Grows on the granite soils of WA.

Pincushion hakea (*Hakea laurina*)
Aboriginal name: Djanda (Nyungar, WA)
Other names: Pinbush, pincushion tree

This shapely shrub or tree grows 2–6 m tall in areas where the summer is hot
and dry. It is one of the best known hakeas and a favourite plant in ornamental bush gardens. The profuse flowers look like creamy-yellow pins
stuck in small round, red pincushions. They are often pollinated by the tiny,
long-snouted and stripe-backed honey possum, found only in WA.

CHAPTER 6

Growing Bushfoods

Taming tucker Growing bushfoods is pleasant and rewarding work. The bushfood garden is a glorious green space, full of delicate flowers, colour, nectar and perfume. It is water-saving, environmentally friendly, low-maintenance and free of chemicals. Best of all, it produces beautiful bush tucker!

Here's how to create a peaceful place where you can sit quietly and get in touch with nature.

The bushfood garden

It's a fallacy to say that native plant gardens are maintenance-free. Plants become woody if not watered and overgrown if not pruned; they can die if they don't get enough water, especially when young, or if they are over-watered or over-fertilised.

Still, bushfood gardens require less upkeep than ordinary gardens (and certainly lawns), so they make ideal gardens for retired people. Once established, most native plants need little work and little water, but, like all plants, respond well to care and attention.

Australian native plants do not like artificial fertilisers. A bushfood garden is natural and organic.

Choose local plants

Local plants contribute to the natural balance of the garden and the whole ecosystem.

Australian plants have adapted to their environment niches over a long time. They are less trouble than exotic plants. Try to obtain local species and varieties which enjoy the soil and climatic conditions of your area. These plants are easier to maintain and will produce well.

Endangered species

Bushfood gardens are a bit like zoos. They bring plants which are threatened with extinction in the wild, due to the destruction of their native habitat, into cultivation. You are helping to ensure their survival.

Well-drained soil

Good drainage is essential for a strong root system and healthy growth. Poor drainage can cause root rot and is a major cause of fatalities in bushfood gardens.

With very few exceptions, the majority of bushfood plants included in this book grow best if there is no excess moisture around their roots for any length of time: they don't like 'wet feet'. This especially applies to plants that grow wild in sandy soils, like those in WA.

In well-drained soil, unlike heavy clay soil, water soaks through the surface and spreads to other levels without being trapped. 'Well-drained' does not mean dry. Plants should receive enough water, but make sure that water does not become stagnant.

Many plant species, like those from rainforests, need a regular supply of moisture. However, in this book, we've included edible plants from all climate zones, including many drought-tolerant species from arid areas.

> **A quick fix**
> To temper **heavy clay** soils, add gypsum at the rate of 1 kg per square metre.
> To temper **light, sandy** soils, dig in well-rotted compost.
> In **badly drained** soils, the best solution is to raise the level of the growing area by making raised beds. See below.

Raised beds

To improve drainage, especially in clay soils, build up garden beds 10 to 20 cm above ground leve and fill them with topsoil.

Raised beds should be about 1 m wide and can be edged or boxed in with logs, sleepers or bush rocks. Curved, round or oval beds have more character than formal square and rectangular ones and winding path-ways are more aesthetic than straight ones.

Add a layer of compost or mulch to the top of the raised bed to prevent the soil surface drying out.

The soil

Organic matter or humus encourages the growth of plants.

Humus is created by fallen leaves and twigs, like the decomposed mass at the bottom of the forest floor. It is part of the continual cycle of life and death in the vegetable world. In fertile soil, thousands of fungi aid decay, helping to break down organic vegetable residues and releasing nutrients to the roots of trees and plants. Humus has two to three times the water-holding capacity of clay.

Many Australian soils are old and leached of nutrients. Those in SA are deficient in phosphorus and in WA they lack manganese. Native plants have adapted to these soil conditions and recycle phosphorus from their old leaves to younger tissue.

Water is precious

Water is a scarce resource. Don't waste it!

Bushfood plants have adapted to their local climate; they conserve water and use it in the most efficient way.

Plants need their water supply deep down in the soil. Established plants whose roots have deeply penetrated the soil can make do with natural rainfall, without extra watering. In arid areas species have strong and deep root systems which can plunge 8 to 10 m to reach water.

A top layer of mulch or compost will conserve moisture by reducing evaporation and because it is porous will allow water to soak into the soil.

Wind can dry out the surface of the soil. Windbreaks of native plants will reduce the water loss.

Watering tips
- Water new bushfood plants twice a week for the first few weeks after planting.
- Water established plants thoroughly, but infrequently. Allow the water to soak right into the soil to the root ball.
- On hot days, water in the late afternoon.
- Conserve water by using a thick covering of **mulch**.
- Buy a rain water tank to save money and be more self-reliant.
- Use watering cans instead of a hose, or use soaker hoses or drip-watering systems.
- Check under mulch to make sure the soil is moist.
- If new tip growth does not wilt, you don't need to water, but water deeply if new growth droops.

Starting out

When establishing your bushfood garden, we suggest that you start with seedlings from a good plant nursery, as many indigenous plants are difficult to propagate from seeds or cuttings.

Grow just a few plants, until you gain some practical experience. Smaller seedling plants, rather than larger ones, have time to adapt to their environment, and grow more strongly.

See the list of suppliers in the **Bushfoods Directory**, p.130. We know you will be impatient to make a start, but first read through the plant profile panels to get a good idea of which plants suit your general climate.

If you are building a house on a bush block, try to keep as many of the plants that are growing on the site as you can. Pot up small shrubs that you have to remove and replant them when your house is built.

Rainforest species

Tropical and subtropical rainforest plants need well-dug, fertile soil for good root growth. They will not succeed in very hard ground.

To loosen the soil, dig over the ground to a depth of 25 to 30 cm and break up any clods in an area of 50 cm around plants and trees. Dig a hole for each plant and allow 1 m diameter of free space around each one. Plant trees 1.5 to 2 m apart.

Don't dig, don't weed

Native plants die if their roots are disturbed. Use mulch.

Don't move dead branches

If they're not in the way, leave dead trees, stumps or branches where they fall. They will decay and provide shelter for small animals like lizards and food for young seedlings.

You can hurry this natural decay by partly covering branches and logs with soil. They will rot and break down into litter, the foundation of the natural bush. This decomposing litter acts like compost or fertiliser.

Mulch

In the bushfood garden, weeding and digging are not needed. Mulch is used to protect plants and feed the soil. Mulch protects plants against the sun. It evens out the ground temperature and smothers 'foreign' weeds.

Don't heap up mulch close to plants. Always spread it outwards and away from bushes and tree trunks.

All sorts of material can be used for mulch.

- Cover garden beds with leaf and bark litter from native plants, gumnuts, dried grass and twigs.
- Add a deep layer of sawdust, wood chips or hardwood shavings.
- Large chips of pine bark are expensive, but a thin layer will last for several years. Pine bark won't blow away, though it can be dislodged by running water.
- Coloured pea gravel, river stones and small pebbles blend nicely into a natural garden.
- Tree prunings and loppings put through a chipper make excellent mulch.
- Sawdust covered with coarse sand is used by some landscape gardeners.

To discourage weeds in an established garden, spread a layer of sand around the plants, then add a 1 cm layer of sawdust, then sprinkle sand on top of it to prevent it blowing away. Wood shavings can be used in the same way.

- Commercial leaf litter is made from chopped-up leaves and offcuts from street tree lopping. You can often buy it cheaply from your local council. It will gradually break down and feed the plants.
- Mulch coastal plants and plants from the inland and SW Australia with sand.

Don't use for mulch
Wood chippings or mulch which contains any camphor laurel, poplar, privet, willow, noxious weeds or timber treated with toxic chemicals.

Living mulch
Ground cover plants provide a living mulch.

Ground-hugging creepers like running postman (*Kennedia prostrata*) form a dense mat (and may have to be cut back harshly). Small prostrate foliage plants such as spreading grevillea or callistemon will attract honey eating birds. Watch your cat!

Fertilisers
Mulch is by far the best fertiliser for bushfood plants but most will respond to natural organic fertilisers, especially when they are at the seedling stage.

Use organic fertilisers like compost or well-rotted, aged, animal manure. Don't use fresh manure or poultry manure which contains too much phosphate and can be toxic to some native plants, especially proteas like banksias and grevilleas.

Blood and bone and low phosphorus, slow-release organic granular fertilisers can be used sparingly when planting and before spring and autumn growth flushes. Try to obtain blood and bone which has no additives. Organic liquid fertilisers are ideal for feeding plants in tubs and other containers.

Compost
Compost is valuable in all soils. It helps to bind light sandy loams and to break up heavy clays. It's easy to make your own compost . Anything that once lived can go into a compost heap. Compost bins are available from

most local councils, or you can make your own compost box using chicken wire, timber planks or pallets.

Once or twice a year, when there is new growth or when fruits form, dig in a spadeful of compost close to the base of trees and shrubs. Or use compost as mulch and spread a thick layer over the whole garden.

Tree branch compost
Make a frame of about 3 sq m using thick tree branches. Fill this box with thin branches and tree prunings. The cellulose-rich material will take 6 to 18 months to break down into a nourishing compost.

Fire pruning
Australian plant species tolerate fire and many are propagated by it.

Shrubs and trees in the bush are 'pruned' by natural outbreaks of fire. Aborigines regularly burnt areas of country to drive small animals into traps and to encourage the fresh growth of lush green grass. This low-intensity fire burnt off leaves and litter.

In desert places, the best flowers and fruits appear after a burn.

Prune bushfood plants?
Most native shrubs benefit from pruning. Pinching back new growth prolongs the life span of plants, so prune each year or every two to three years.

Lightly prune plants especially those in a pot so they don't become spindly, overgrown or leggy. Pinch out the tips during the growing season.

Prune after a new flush of spring growth, then water well. Don't prune when plants are dormant.

Pruning will promote flowering of species which flower on young wood. If you grow banksias to produce cut flowers, plants should be pruned regularly and heavily.

Start to prune trees and shrubs when they are young. You can't shape older trees. The plants can be clipped or pruned to create hedges.

To tip-prune, use your fingernails to pinch or pull off about 1 cm of the growing tip of each branch. This forces the growth of side shoots lower down the branches and bushes out the plants.

Use clippers for larger shrubs and trees and cut leafless wood back as much as 10 cm.

Water plants well after pruning. Use all your tree prunings for **mulch.**

Propagating bushfood plants

Once your bushfood garden is established, you will have time to experiment and grow plants from your own seeds and cuttings, or from those you swap with friends.

Most indigenous trees and shrubs can be propagated from seeds. Many are easy to grow, some are fiddly, and a few are very difficult.

Collecting seeds

The easiest seeds to collect are those from fruits like lilly pillies and gee-bungs. The whole fruit ripens and falls from the plant. Collect them and allow them to dry before planting. To speed up germination, leave fruit to ferment in a small amount of water for a few days, then wash or rub the flesh from the seed before planting.

Crack and remove the woody shell around seeds of plants like quandongs.

Plant your seeds, or allow them to dry and store them in paper envelopes or bags. Seeds of some plants are contained in hard seed cases that stay on the plant, sometimes for several years. Three types are common: capsules, follicles and pods.

Mature seed capsules of callistemon (bottlebrushes), leptospermums (tea-trees) and melaleucas (paperbarks) are dry and woody and split in several places to release large quantities of small, fine seed. Put unopened capsules in a warm place or leave them in the sun until they dry and split open to release the seeds. This may take from days to weeks. Plant or store seeds.

Banksias, hakeas and gre-villeas bear woody follicles, which are similar to capsules, but have one major split along their side. The large seeds with papery wings are dispersed by the wind. One way of removing

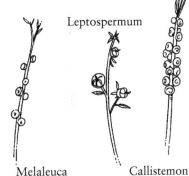

Banksia   Melaleuca   Leptospermum   Callistemon

the seeds is to burn the follicle in a fire or hold it over a naked flame for a few seconds and then plunge it into water.

Grevillea seeds are easily released from their follicles without any treatment.

Treatment

Acacias (wattles) and running postman produce pea-like pods which, when dry, split along two edges to release their hard-coated seeds.

For successful germination, seeds should be softened. This is usually done by scarification — removing part of the seed coat by scratching or nicking the seed with a razor blade or sharp knife or by rubbing it with coarse sandpaper.

Otherwise, immerse the seeds in hot water, just off the boil, for a few minutes, then put into cold water and allow to soak for several hours until they swell. Many native plant seeds germinate more easily if soaked in water overnight before planting.

The seeds are usually sown in spring or autumn and most should germinate within 10 to 20 days. Grevillea seeds may take several months. Sow fine seeds in a good potting mix in cartons, plastic pots, trays or other containers and cover them lightly with sand or mulch.

Larger seeds can be sown in individual pots or directly into the garden. Water seedlings gently and frequently.

Cuttings

Cuttings are taken from the stems or tips of healthy growing plants. It's best to take cuttings when it's cool. They often flower more quickly than plants grown from seeds.

Plant them in a potting mix in plastic pots at least 6 cm deep. Dipping the cut end in a hormone powder will speed up rooting. On average, roots take three or four months to develop, but difficult plants can take up to a year.

Potting mixes for cuttings
1. Coarse washed river sand or sieved bush sand
2. 50/50 sand and peat moss
3. 50/50 sand and vermiculite
4. 75/25 sand and peat moss or compost

Tip and stem cuttings

Use a sharp knife. Choose a piece of stem, usually the growing tip of the plant, about 6 to 10 cm long. Cut below a leaf node or joint, making a straight cut across the stem. Remove most of the leaves.

Dip the cutting into water, then into powdered hormone rooting compound (HRC). Make a hole in the potting mix using a pencil or small stick. Push in the cutting, firm the soil and water well.

Softwood cuttings

Softwood cuttings are taken from semi-hard wood when the current season is complete. Select healthy stems 8 to 15 cm long. Cut just below where the leaves meet the stem. Remove all leaves except two at the top. Insert cuttings in the pots and water well.

Softwood cuttings strike well in humid conditions such as a greenhouse.

Half-hard cuttings

To propagate acacias (wattles), take 5 cm cuttings of half-hard wood and put them to root in a warm place. Tubes rather than pots are best for trees like acacias which form taproots.

Root division

When plants are nearing the end of their productive life, or become too big for their spot, they can be propagated by root division.

Lift the plant carefully. Break the roots apart, so that each part has some leaves and stems. One way to do this is to put two garden forks into a root clump and rock them, easing the two halves apart. Neaten the edges with clippers.

Design

We think bushfood gardens should be informal, just like the bush. Keep your garden simple and natural, with winding paths and walkways, stone steps and borders and timber decks.

A small, semi-circular garden is attractive and easy to maintain and ideal for a backyard. The tallest trees or shrubs should go at the centre rear and have plants arranged in descending order of height in a semi-circle around them.

The key to creating a bushfood garden is to reproduce the original natural landscape of your area, which was there before your house was built. So, look at the bush in your area, or take a walk in your nearest national park to get some ideas and inspiration. Try to include a cross section of the major local species of bushfoods.

Design tips

- Make sure you allow room for a few plants for colour and fragrance and to attract birds.
- Add interest by varying the heights of your trees and shrubs to ensure different levels. You can create walls of climbing foliage and flowers (appleberries or five corners) and hedges of flowering plants (banksias and melaleucas), make a floor of low ground cover (muntries or pigface) and a roof canopy of bushfruits (lilly pillies).
- Plant in clumps or groups, rather than in straight lines.
- Take note of the colours in your garden. You could paint your house roof in similar colours to your plants.
- It's nice to be able to see the garden from the house.
- Hide telegraph poles and fence posts by placing bushfood plants in front of them.
- If you live in the country, plant local species around the perimeter of your property to bring the bush into the garden.
- Plan ahead to prevent bushfire hazards by ensuring that when trees are fully grown they won't overhang your roof or drop leaves or bark into the gutters. Take any electric wires into account.
- Allow room for tree roots to spread. Keep them away from underground cables and water and sewerage pipes.
- A dense buffer zone of bushfood plants between your house and the street will cut down traffic noises and pollution and provide shade and privacy.

Planting schemes

When planning your bushfood garden, you should take into account the height, space and position (full sun or shade) needed by each plant and also the appearance, colour and scent of the foliage and flowers.

You want the garden to look pretty throughout the year, so select species that flower and fruit at different times. You'll also want a balance of bushfruits, bushleaf flavours, vegetables, nuts, seed, tea and nectar plants. Always choose local species because they obviously thrive in your area.

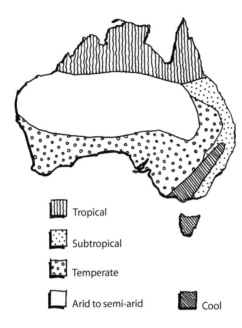

Tropical

Subtropical

Temperate

Arid to semi-arid

Cool

Major climatic zones of Australia

Dig up the lawn!

If you have a problem finding space for a bushfood garden, it could be solved by digging up the lawn. It will also help you save water.

In Australia's cities and suburbs, 25 to 30 per cent of the domestic water supply goes through sprinklers and hoses to keep foreign 'English' lawns green in the searing heat of summer. Scarce fossil fuels are used in lawn fertilisers and weedicides and as petrol in lawn mowers. Then there is all the work and effort of mowing, weeding, trimming and watering.

Dig up the lawn. Turn over the clods of grass and place them on the top of the soil and allow them to die and form a mulch. Collect dead leaves, pine needles, bark, soft rotting wood, gumnuts and pebbles and spread them thickly on the area you want to plant.

We hope that one day bushfood gardens will replace grass lawns as the symbol of suburbia.

Bushfoods Directory

SUPPLIERS

We've compiled this updated list of Australian nurseries and mail order suppliers specialising in bushfood plants, seeds and nuts. You can phone for further information, search for suppliers and catalogues online, or send a stamped, self-addressed envelope to enquire by mail.

A.C.T.

Australian Native Plants Society, Canberra Region, PO Box 217 Civic Square 2068. Two plant sales each year in March and October.

Seeds and Plants Australia, 8 Beltana Road, Piallago 2609 (PO Box 4001, Ainslie 2602). Phone (02) 6247 7180. Nursery open Monday to Friday.

New South Wales

Blacktown Council Nursery, Kent Street, Blacktown 2148. Phone (02) 9839 6000.

City of Randwick Community Nursery, 2B Barker Street, Kingsford 2032. Phone (02) 9399 0933.

Cornucopia Nursery, 55 Station Street, Mullumbimby 2482. Phone (02) 6684 3811.

Dealbata Cold Climate Australian Plant Nursery, (Off) Bloomfield Street, Dalgety 2628. Phone (02) 6456 5043.

Harvest Seeds & Native Plants, 281 Mona Vale Road (PO Box 325), Terrey Hills 2084. Phone (02) 9450 2699.

Koala Native Plants, Branxton 2335. Phone (02) 4938 3380. Mail order.

Ku-ring-gai Council Community Nursery, 430 Mona Vale Road, St. Ives 2075. Phone (02) 9424 0376.

Mole Station Native Plant Nursery, Mole Station, Tenterfield 2372. Phone (02) 6737 5429.

Muru Mittigar Nursery, 89-151 Old Castlereagh Road (LPO Box 7075), South Penrith 2750.

Rainforest Seed Collective, PMB, Bellingen 2454. Phone (02) 6655 2233

Randwick City Council Community Nursery, 2B Barker Street (Corner Day Lane and Barker Street), Kingsford 2032. Phone (02) 9399 0933.

South Coast Flora, 146 Dignam's Creek Rd, via Cobargo 2550. Phone (02) 6493 6747.

The Sydney Rainforest, PO Box 259, Ourimbah 2258. Phone (02) 4362 2499. Phone (02) 9548 2818.

Sydney Wildflower Nursery, 9 Veno Street, Heathcote 2233. No mail order.

Terania Rainforest Nursery, Main Arm Road (PO Box 850),

Mullumbimby 2482. Phone (02) 6684 3100.

Wariapendi Nursery, 33 Church Avenue, Colo Vale 2575. Phone (02) 4889 4092.

Weereewa Native Plants, 35 Rutledge Street, Bungendore 2621. Phone (02) 6238 1794.

Northern Territory

Alice Springs Desert Park Nursery, Larapinta Drive (PO Box 1120), Alice Springs 0871. Phone (08) 8951 8740.

Inland Nursery, PO Box 2065, Alice Springs. Phone (08) 8953 0655.

Ironstone Lagoon Nursery, 69 Lagoon Road, Knuckey's Lagoon (GPO Box 25), Darwin 0801. Phone (08) 8984 3186.

Karguru Nursery, Lot 2052, Staunton Street, Tennant Creek 0860. Phone (08) 8962 2163.

Queensland

Baroondah Station Nursery, Stork Street, Longreach 4730. Phone (0427) 581 289.

Bowerbird Native Nursery, 584 Kingsford Smith Drive, Hamilton 4007. Phone (07) 3216 4209.

Barung Native Plant Nurseries, Shop 3, Riverside Centre (PO Box 1074) Maleny 4552. Phone (07) 5494 3151.

Bush Nuts Native Nursery, 64 Syndicate Road, Tallebudgera Valley 4228. Phone (0448) 253 396.

Fairhill Native Plants, Fairhill Road, Yandina 4561. Phone (07) 5446 8644.

Longreach Bush Tucker, 135 Wren Street, Longreach 4730. Phone (07) 4658 3873.

Neilson's Native Nursery, 49-51 Beenleigh-Redland Bay Road, Loganholme 4129. Phone (07) 3171 2816.

Soul-Lee Native Flora, 25 Foxton Street, Bundamba, Ipswich 4304. Phone (07) 3389 3355. Open Thursday to Sunday.

South Coast Flora, 146 Dignams Creek Road, Cobargo 2550. Phone (02) 6493 6747.

Toona Rainforest Gardens, 12 Pharlap Avenue, Mudgeeraba 4213. Phone (07) 5530 5299.

Yeppoon Rainforest Nursery, Adelaide Park Road (PO Box 109), Yeppoon 4703. Phone (07) 4939 3963.

Yuruga Nursery, Kennedy Highway, Walkamin 4872. Phone (07) 4093 3826.

Wijuti Grub Bushfood Nursery, 264 Walli Creek Road (PO Box 171), Kenilworth 4574. Phone (07) 5446 0264

South Australia

Australian Bush Products, PO Box 131, Strathalbyn 5255. Phone (08) 8532 2698.

Perry's Fruit & Nut Nursery, Kangarilla Road, McLaren Flat 5171. Phone (08) 8383

0268. Suppliers of Bunya and Macadamia nuts, Quendong and Native Lime.

State Flora Nurseries, Upper Sturt Road, Belair National Park 5052. Phone (08) 8278 777. National Park entry fee refunded if you only visit the nursery.

State Flora Nursery, Bremer Road, Murray Bridge. 5253. Phone (08) 8539 2105.

Tasmania

Habitat Plants, 240 Jones Road, Liffey 7302. Phone (03) 6397 3400. Retail Friday to Monday.

Plants of Tasmania, 65 Hall Street, Ridgeway 7054. Phone (03) 6239 1583. Closed Saturday.

Wildseed Tasmania, 91 Weston Hill Road, Sorell 7172. Phone (03) 6265 2651.

Woodbridge Nursery, PO Box 90, Woodbridge 7162. Phone (0438) 674 437. Open Friday and Saturday.

Victoria

Austplant Nursery and Gardens, 249 Purves Road, Arthurs Seat 3936. Phone (03) 5989 6120.

Candlebark Community Nursery, Hull Road near Taylor Road, Mooroolbark; PO Box 6064, Croydon North 3136. Phone (03) 9727 0549.

Ceres Permaculture & Bushfood Nursery, Roberts & Stewart Streets, Brunswick East 3057.

Phone (03) 9389 0111.

Ficifolia Native Nursery, 455 Main South Road, Drouin South 3818. Phone (03) 5627 6457.

Geelong Indigenous Nurseries Network, 50 Coppards Road, Newcomb 3219. Phone (0425) 752 648.

Gippsland Indigenous Plants, Dow Road, Valencia Creek 3860. Phone (03) 5154 4468.

Kuranga Native Nursery, 118 York Road Mount Evelyn 3796. Phone (03) 9760. 8100. Paperbark Cafe.

Lang's Native Plant Nursery, 564 Eleventh Street, Mildura 3500. Phone (03) 5023 2551.

Peppermint Ridge Farm Nursery, PO Box 42, Tynong North 3818. Phone (03) 5942 8580.

St. Kilda Indigenous Nursery Co-operative, 525 Williamstown Road, Port Melbourne 3207. Phone (03) 9645 2477.

Victorian Indigenous Nurseries Co-Operative, Yarra Bend Road, Fairfield (off Heidelberg Road), 3078. Closed weekends.

Wimmera Native Nursery, PO Box 98, Dimboola 3414. Phone (03) 5389 1193.

Western Australia

Australian Native Nurseries Group, w141 King Road, Oakford 6121. Phone (08) 9525 1324.

Australian Wildflower Seeds, PO Box 3139, Carlisle South (Perth) 6101. Phone (08) 9470 6999.

Geographe Community Landcare
  Nursery, 366 Queen Elizabeth
  Avenue (PO Box 798), Busselton
  6280. Open Monday and Tuesday.
Lullfitz Nursery, PO Box 34,
  Wanneroo 6946. Phone (08) 9405
  1607.
Native Nursery, 18 Possum Place,
  Busselton 6280. Phone (08) 9751
  1427.
Nindetharna Seed Service, PO Box
  2121, Albany 6331. Phone (08) 9844
  3573.

BUSHFOODS GARDENS
Australian Capital Territory
Aboriginal Trail, Australian National
  Botanic Gardens, Clunies Ross
  Street, Canberra, ACT 2600. Part
  of the National Botanical Gardens.
  A well-marked trail leads through
  various climatic regions, with signs
  identifying plants and explanations
  about them. Phone: (02) 6250 9540.

New South Wales
Gadyn Walking Track, Berry Island
  Reserve, near Balls Head Bay,
  North Sydney. A walk through quiet
  remnant Sydney Harbour bushland.
  A gesture of reconciliation by North
  Sydney Council to the Camaraigal
  people of northern Sydney.
Ku-ring-gai Wild Flower Garden,
  420 Mona Vale Road, St Ives
  (Sydney), NSW. Walking tracks over
  100 ha of natural bush and new
  native plantings. Open daily from
  10 a.m. Nursery, Monday to Friday.

La Perouse Bush Tucker
  Information Walk, La Perouse
  (Sydney). Maintained by trainees
  who began to study bush tucker
  plants and clear weed infestation at
  La Perouse in February 1997. They
  were taught by John Lennis.
Mt Annan Botanical Gardens, Mt.
  Annan Drive, Mount Annan, NSW
  2567, via Camden. Open daily from
  10 a.m. Occasional guided walks
  through bushfoods garden. Phone:
  (02) 4648 2477
Royal Botanical Gardens, Sydney,
  Mrs Macquarie's Road, Sydney.
  Australian plants garden near
  the herbarium which includes
  bushfoods. Phone: (02) 9231 8111
Stony Range Flora Reserve,
  Pittwater Road, Dee Why
  (Sydney), NSW. Open Monday
  to Sunday, 10 a.m. to 4 p.m. A
  hilly site, covering 3.5 hectares of
  Hawkesbury sandstone country.
  Local species and native plants from
  different parts of Australia.
Summerland House With No
  Steps, 3 km south of Alstonville,
  northen NSW. The NSW
  Department of Agriculture has
  established a bushfruit garden of 384
  trees, covering 35 species, including
  sandpaper fig, beach cherry, bopple
  nuts and the endangered smooth
  Davidson's plum as part of a botanic
  garden.
Wirrimbirra Sanctuary, David G.
  Stead Memorial Wildlife Research
  Foundation of Australia, Hume

Highway, Bargo. Nursery, books and wildflower garden. Open daily.

Northern Territory

Alice Springs Desert Park,
Larapinta Drive, Alice Springs, NT. Open daily, 7.30 a.m.–6 p.m. Spectacular plant habitats and animal exhibit show that the desert is rich, varied and full of life. Phone: (08) 8951 8788.

Olive Pink Botanic Garden, Tuncks Road, Alice Springs, NT. Open daily, 10 a.m.–6 p.m. Arid zone botanical gardens established by Olive Pink (1884–1975), who from the 1930s lived and studied with the Aborigines of the Tanami Desert. Visitor Centre with bushfoods displays. Phone: (08) 8952 2154.

Queensland

Aboriginal Plant Use Garden,
Flecker Botanic Gardens, Cairns City Council, Collins Avenue, Cairns, Qld. Open each day from 7.30 a.m. to 5.30 p.m. The garden includes edible food plants and also plants used by Aborigines for fibre, weapons, utensils, shelter and water. Phone: (07) 4044 3398.

Redlands IndigiScape, Capalaba (20km south east of Brisbane). A demonstration garden over 14 ha, including eco systems, plants, flowers, lakes and natural bush.

South Australia

Shoalmarra Quandong Farm,
Thuruna Road, Tumby Bay, SA 5605. Tours of the farm. Products for sale include quandong jam and dried fruit. Phone: (08) 8688 2546.

Victoria

Bush Tucker Garden, Native Garden, Department of Ecology and Evolutionary Biology, Monash University, Clayton, Melbourne, Vic. Display of native plants, including bushfoods. Phone the curator Johann de Bree: (03) 9905 4000.

Western Australia

Banksia Farm, Mount Barker. The only garden in Australia where you can find all 73 varieties of nectar yielding banksia, of which 58 are indigenous to the SW of Australia.

Kings Park and Botanic Garden,
Perth Flora of Western Australia

Australian Plants Society
(formerly The Society for Growing Australian Plants) This active group encourages growing and using Australian native plants in home gardens and public places. They also promote study of native plants and their habitats and publish useful books and newsletters. There are local branches throughout Australia. To find your local group, contact Australian Plants Society at:
Mail: PO Box 744, Blacktown 2148
Phone: (02) 9621 3437 Fax: (02) 9676 7603
Internet homepage:
www.ozemail.com.au/~sgap

BUSHFOODS BIBLIOGRAPHY

Aboriginal People of Central Australia. *Desert Bush Tucker Identikit. Common Native Food Plants of Central Australia.* Parks and Wildlife Commission of the Northern Territory, Alice Springs, 1995.

Albrecht, Rev. F. W. *The Natural Food Supply of the Australian Aborigines* [Hermannsburg]. Adelaide, 1947.

Bailey, F. Manson. 'Edible fruits indigenous to Queensland'. *Queensland Agricultural Journal* (vol. 2, part 6). Brisbane, 1898. *Comprehensive Catalogue of Queensland Plants*. Brisbane, 1909.

Bancroft, J. 'Food of the Aborigines of Central Australia'. *Proceedings of the Royal Society of Queensland* (vol. 1, part 111). Brisbane, 1884.

Bates, Daisy. *The Native Tribes of Western Australia* [1904–12]. White, Isobel (ed.). Canberra, 1985.

Bindon, Peter. *Useful Bush Plants.* W. A. Museum, Perth, 1996.

Brough-Smyth, R. *The Aborigines of Victoria*. Melbourne, 1876.

Bruneteau, Jean-Paul. *Tukka: Real Australian Food*. Pymble, 1996.

Cherikoff, Vic. The Bush Food Handbook, Sydney, 1989.

Cooper, Wendy (ed.) and Cooper, Warren T. (illustrator). *Fruits of the Rain Forest*. Chatswood, NSW, 1994.

Crawford, I. M. (ed.). *Traditional Aboriginal plant resources in the Kalumbura area: Aspects in ethno-economics*. Records of the Western Australian Museum, Supp. No. 15. Perth, 1982.

Cribb, A.B. & J. W. *Wild Food in Australia*. Sydney, 1981 (1974).

Daw, Brad *et al. Bush Tucker. Plants of the South-West*. Department of Conservation and Land Management (CALM), Como, 1997.

Dawson, James. *Australian Aborigines*. Melbourne, 1881.

Gibson, Athol and Knight, Eric. *Bourke Bush Foods. Traditional Foods of the Bourke Aboriginal People*. Bourke (NSW), c. 1986.

Gott, Beth and Zola, Nelly. *Koorie Plants, Koorie People*. Melbourne, 1992.

Henderson, John. *Excursions and Adventures in New South Wales*. London, 1851 (2 vols.).

House, A. P. N. and Harwood, C.E. (eds). *Australian Dry-zone Acacias for Human Food*. Australian Tree Centre, CSIRO, East Melbourne, 1992.

Isaacs, Jennifer. *Bush Food. Aboriginal food and herbal medicine*. Sydney, 1996 (1987).

Lands, Merrilee. *Mayi: some bush*

fruits of Dampierland. Mambulantjin Aboriginal Corporation, Broome, 1989.

Latz, Peter. Bushfires and Bushtucker: Aboriginal Plant Use in Central Australia. Alice Springs, 1995.

Levitt, Dulcie. Plants and People. Aboriginal uses of plants on Groote Eylandt. AIAS, Canberra, 1981.

Low, Tim. Bush Tucker: Australia's Wild Food Harvest. Pymble, 1992.

Macarthur, William and Moore, Charles. Catalogue des Collections de Bois Indigènes des différents districts de cette colonie. NSW Australie. L'Exposition de 1855, Paris.

Maiden, Joseph. The Useful Native Plants of Australia. Sydney, 1889.

Nicholson, Nan and Hugh. Australian Rainforest Plants. The Channon (4 vols), 1992–4.

Radke, Peter and Ann and Sankowsky, Garry and Nada. Growing Australian Tropical Plants. Malanda, 1993.

Robins, Juleigh. Wild Lime: Cooking from the bushfood garden. St Leonards, 1996.

Roth, Walter, E. Food: Its search, capture, and preparation. North Queensland Ethnology: Bulletin No.3. Brisbane, 1901.

Sainsbury, R. M. A Field Guide to Dryandras. Nedlands, 1985.

Stewart, Kathy and Percival, Bob. Bush Foods of New South Wales. A botanic record of an Aboriginal oral history. Royal Botanic Gardens, Sydney, 1997.

Turner, Margaret Mary. Arrernte Foods from Central Australia. Illustrated by Shawn Dobson. Institute for Aboriginal Development, Alice Springs, 1994.

Welsby, Thomas. 'Recollections of the Natives of Moreton Bay'. Historical Society Journal (vol. 1, no. 3). Brisbane, August 1917.

Wightman, Glenn and Brown, Jessie. Jaywon Plant Identikit. Common useful plants in the Katherine area of northern Australia. Jaywon Association, Katherine, 1994.

Wrigley, John and Fagg, Murray. Australian Native Plants. Sydney, 1997 (1979).

INDEX OF PLANTS

INDEX OF RECIPES AND USES